NEW FOR 1987

THESE TWO NEW GUIDES are full of indispensable information for anyone wishing to play golf or go fishing whilst away from home. They contain details of golf clubs and fishing grounds which welcome visitors and nearby hotels which can cater for them and provide all the facilities they need. With other interesting information and features and tips from such celebrities as Tony Jacklin, Jack Charlton and Trevor Housby, these guides will make it easy to plan your golf or fishing trip and be assured of a welcome at a convenient hotel.

England for Golf and England for Fishing are published by Pastime Publications in association with the English Tourist Board and will be on sale from January 1987. They cost £1.10 each and are available from all good bookshops or by post, price £1.50 each (inc p&p), from:

Pastime Publications Ltd, 15 Dublin Street Lane South, Edinburgh EH1 3PX.

(Please make cheques payable to Pastime Publications Ltd.)

AVAILABLE January 1987

CONTENTS

Pastime Publications Ltd gratefully acknowledge the assistance of The Scottish Tourist Board, Area Tourist Boards, The A.A., The Royal and Ancient Golf Club of St. Andrews and the United States Golf Association and others in compiling this guide.

Published by Pastime Publications Limited, 15 Dublin Street Lane South, Edinburgh EH1 3PX. Tel: 031-556 1105/0057.

First published by The Scottish Tourist Board 1970

Typesetting by Newtext Composition Ltd.
Printed & Bound by G.A. Pindar & Son Ltd.
U.K. Distribution by W.H.S. Distributors

Worldwide distribution by
The British Tourist Authority

INDEX

The Home of Golf – St. Andrews.
The closing scenes at the 1984 Open Championship at the Old Course.

SCOTLAND
FOR
GOLF

BY MALCOLM CAMPBELL

Previous page, Comrie Golf Course, Tayside. Above. The New Course, St. Andrews, Fife.

Scotland is the traditional home of the royal and ancient game of golf and within its borders lies a golfing paradise of more than 400 courses without peer anywhere on the globe. What follows is but a mere taste of the golfing delights of the nation which gave the game to the world.

Few, if any, have tasted them all, but Scotland extends a warm welcome to all who would try.

MALCOLM CAMPBELL

THE LURE
OF THE SCOTTISH LINKS

BY NICOLAS PARK

GOLF, roughly speaking, can last as long as life. Years after the footballer and the cricketer hang up their boots, the golfer goes on. Even if his handicap goes up, to play golf worse than he used to do is surely better than to play not at all.

And anyone who plays golf, seriously or otherwise, must at some time in his life find himself heading for Scotland to pay homage in the country where it all began. In fact until he does there is no doubt in my mind that he has not come of age in a golfing sense. This remark is not due to an excess of patriotic zeal for I am not Scottish; so I shall do my best to make clear the reasons for my confident assertion. They are many and diverse; certainly a flying visit to the nearest souvenir shop in St. Andrews does not fit the bill! Our greatest golfing scribe, Bernard Darwin, put it all very well when, long ago, he wrote an introduction to a piece describing the charms of St. Andrews:

"When I was in America I was asked by a golfer who had never been in Scotland, what was the difference between St. Andrews and an ordinary, good, machine made inland course. I do not remember what I answered, but I am sure I did not make him even faintly understand."

In a few simple words he thus elevated to its rightful place not only the home of golf but also the distinctive form of the game that is played there. Links golf. The game that was born in Scotland and played there on many sites for centuries before any other country took it up. These two aspects of the game — the links sites and the type of golf played on them demand your attention and need to be thought about in a little more detail. Understand them and you will know the game itself much better. And you will truly realise why Scotland is the home of golf — and why so many people return year after year to enjoy its attractions.

THE early Scottish game was played at over a dozen different places, of which St. Andrews was but one. These were all sited on the eastern seaboard of Scotland, at towns such as Dornoch, Montrose, Barry, Scotscraig, St. Andrews, Elie, Leven, Musselburgh, North Berwick and Dunbar. The description "link" was given to that piece of land connecting the beach with more stable land inshore. It is, in fact, derived from a word meaning "ridge" which gives a clue to the type of ground to be found on a links. Along certain parts of our island coastline, the sea has receded and left a series of sandy wastes composed of bold ridges and significant furrows. The action of our climate — principally the wind — has then shaped these forms into dunes and hollows of varying height, width and depth.

The first vegetation to colonise this harsh environment are the marram and lyme grasses, coarse plants whose roots help at first to bind the sand together. After the initial stabilisation come the finer bent and fescue grasses which establish the thick, close growing, hard-wearing sward that is such a feature of true links turf wherever it is found.

Finally, in due course, come the higher forms of vegetation where conditions are more sheltered: heather, whins (gorse), broom and a few trees, particularly as one moves inland.

This variety of terrain and vegetation attracted and sustained a wide variety of animal life. Especially significant were the rabbits, which grazed on the grasses and kept them cropped short. Some links even became known as "warrens" or "burrows" and in them both the foxes and man hunted their prey. And when eventually man, the sportsman, having adopted golf as a pastime, went in search of suitable ground he found it waiting for him almost ready to hand. Primitive land by today's reckoning but it exactly supplied the fundamental and traditional characteristic of golfing terrain.

UNDULATION, it has been said, is the soul of golf and links terrain supplies this in abundance. One of the great characteristics of golf is that it offers — or should — a challenge to the sportsman in working out how to play any particular stroke. Ground of almost infinitely variable slope is particularly attractive for use in a game that employs a round ball. By contrast, try playing golf on a flattish sports ground and see what a dull game it becomes.

However, there was much more to this developing game than the mental processes involved in combating undulation. There was the climate itself, which can change by the minute on the seashore. Most variable was the wind — it's strength and direction. And then there was the effect of rain in softening the ground, so that shots played in the air to avoid obstacles would stop more quickly near the target. Conversely, periods of summer drought left the ground baked hard, during which time running shots became more effective and necessary.

Terrain, climate — the list of variables is not finished for there was one effect of the vegetation itself. Was the grass near the hole cropped short or were there patches of longer stuff between ball and cup? How to avoid those whins or this swathe of heather?

As the first golfers explored the possibilities of their new game, they gradually found favourite routes — the early holes — which seemed to offer the best test, the "most sporting challenge" that their links had to offer. Over centuries, their rules and courses have become enshrined in golfing lore and that is to be expected. Golf stood the test of time — as a mental and physical test of skill. And even, to some extent, as a game of chance in which the bad breaks evened out with the good ones over a period of time.

Which makes it all the more difficult to understand why this original version of the game should increasingly be regarded as simply a throwback to the past. Man, quite naturally, having invented such an ingenious pastime, has sought to improve on his brainchild. In the process of doing this it seems to me that he has simply tried to remove many of the variables which went to make up the charm of the original game.

FOR a start, he convinced himself he could move the game inland. In Britain this worked up to a point, especially on sites that were in reality old links stranded inland during previous geological upheavals. Then came the architects who would lay out a "golf" course on virtually any bit of spare ground and gradually golfers convinced themselves that their "inland" game was a valid copy of its ancestor. And the game did not stop in Britain: such an attractive pastime moved to other countries, notably America. Here the original parameters of the game became even more blurred — undulation was supplemented and even submerged by trees and lakes; climate was much more "consistent"; and different grasses grew, on which the ball behaved very differently.

All this change in the game is history and I do not particularly mean to condemn any of it. But I do feel very strongly that we should be much more aware of the heritage that is left in Scotland. We need to become much better at preserving it. Not just for the sake of history — it is actually a working heritage because on many of these sites it is still possible to play a game very similar to the original. The undulation is still there; and the climatic variations; and not infrequently the vegetation is the same. The same grasses are being carefully maintained at not a few sites, as is the challenge of "low-scrub habitat" like gorse, broom and heather. But beware: do not expect to play the same game very well if you go armed with "distance" golf balls and thick-soled clubs designed for the fleshly grasses of American courses. The Scottish game demands implements of feel and judgement, balls which allow subtle skills and finesse to be exercised. Choose your weapons with care, for this game on the links is one of brawn **and** brain, of patience and fortitude and skill and courage. But the rewards

Continued on page 6

The Medal Course, Montrose, Tayside.
Please mention this Pastime Publications guide.

in terms of satisfaction and relaxation are, I believe, proportionately much greater than can be found on so many of the mechanical, consistent, target courses that pass as tests of golf in this age of "improvement".

The ordinary, good machine made inland courses that Bernard Darwin wrote about so many years ago is now such a common beast throughout the world that we must constantly remind ourselves just what constitutes perfection and excellence so far as the game and its courses are concerned.

So just where shall we go to find this wonderful game? And when? For those who have been in St. Andrews during the busy July and August these are pertinent questions indeed. Let me offer a few thoughts on these problems, which are in themselves rather delightful ones to solve.

PLANNING a golfing holiday is, in common with most other holidays, an enjoyable exercise against which the only thing to be said is that we shall never enjoy it quite as much as we imagine. The moment of packing our clubs will always be more exquisite than any we shall enjoy in the using of them. In short, "to travel hopefully is better than to arrive."

Even so, the great day does arrive and when might it be? Well, that rather depends on how much golf you wish to play and where you want to play it. If you must go to St. Andrews on long, crowded summer days then certainly you will experience a fierce struggle for life, the hope, too often disappointed, of getting a number in the ballot. And the despair and sense of waste in having to go on to the New Course or Eden or Jubilee (fine courses in their own right though they may be). Yet go to St. Andrews in winter and you will

scarcely know the place. Start on whatever course you will, as early as you will and try to play two rounds before the dark falls. Then in the early evening sit round the roaring fire in hotel or clubhouse and you will feel much more a part of this ancient town than during its cosmopolitan summer season.

This, then, is one of the beauties of the British climate: the tolerable day can be found and enjoyed at any season of the year. What can be better than autumn, if we banish from our minds the fact that winter is coming? Then again, I think of the many sunny winter days on the links with the greens neither fast nor slow, the holes playing at their ideal length. A wind just strong enough to make me feel cleverer in playing it than I really am. Yet inevitably this is followed by perhaps the best day of all, in springtime, when we can even dash out for a few holes or a few shots after tea.

So the "when" is perhaps of less consequence than the "where." And here the choice is thrilling: I can bring to mind at least 40 great links in Scotland where I would be delighted to settle down for a week's golf. Links where golf can, at most times of the year, be played in perfect peace and at no great cost. And am I going to describe them to you? No, I am not, for perhaps the greatest delight that golf has offered me has been the chance to discover them for myself. It really is not too difficult: given that you are in Scotland and set your stall out to play links golf, you do not need the wit of Sherlock Holmes to find your own paradise. Or paradises. And when you do hit on favourite spots, it will be an interesting test of character to see if you share the information with your friends!

Ailsa Craig standing twelve miles out to sea from Turnberry.

BUT a few clues at least may grudgingly be offered. As you shoot past Carlisle on the M6 and A74, have you not thought to turn on to the A75, and head for Southerness? There you will find a course sited on the savage Solway firth, and look back to the dark Galloway hills or across the Firth to the English Lake District.

And crossing through Stewart country, you hit the Atlantic coast at Turnberry, eyes drawn to Ailsa Craig standing twelve miles out in the bay. Not far away, you must play Prestwick and experience "the long table". The historian knows he is on hallowed ground there.

From next door at Troon I once drove the best part of 200 miles to my next course. Machrihanish stands on the Mull of Kintrye, looking across to Ireland. It must surely be the least accessible of all the famous courses on the British mainland, yet that is a particular part of its charm. If you cannot enjoy the drive past Loch Lomond into Argyllshire then you should not be in Scotland anyway!

Such a remark highlights yet another bonus which is the golfer's lot in Scotland. There is so much magnificent scenery to enjoy, a factor which the Scots themselves are apt to overlook. As you drive up to Dornoch — as one day you surely must — the spectacular A9 road allows you to see much of the Cairngorms, with mountain tops frequently covered in snow giving a feeling of the raw power of Nature. Here too you will see Golden Eagle and Osprey without being especially observant — and surely you will notice and may visit, the famous Highland malt whisky distilleries whose labels you see all over the world — Glenfiddich, The Glenlivet, The Macallan, Glenmorangie. The last named was Henry Longhurst's favourite tipple; as you drive on the high road over the Black Isle you can see the loch from which the water is

Gullane in East Lothian has several fine courses including Muirfield.

drawn to make it. At the same moment Dornoch Firth unfolds below you and very soon you are surveying one of the great golfing panoramas. Looking back to the great hills of Sutherland and forwards to the Firth, to Dornoch Sands and a great golf course.

Heading south you cannot miss Nairn, or a string of links along the Moray Firth (neither too should you miss Cawdor Castle, one of Scotlands great ancestral homes). Drive through Speyside and Royal Deeside and you are nearing many great courses, of which Carnoustie and St. Andrews are simply the best known. And still the scenery is to be enjoyed, for you have reached the Firth of Forth, and Edinburgh, always my favourite city. And you still have to sample Gullane, Muirfield and North Berwick,

overlooked by that peculiar hump of rock called North Berwick Law.

There now, I think I have not given too much away — barely a dozen courses mentioned out of a possible forty or more. At all these places — at virtually any time of year — you can still play and enjoy the classic game of golf. Having referred to Bernard Darwin at the beginning, let me finish with a little more of his wisdom:

"If I wrote for a year I could not hope to convey the charm of St. Andrews to those who have not been there, and those who have been need no telling." For St. Andrews, read Scotland and you have the thing in a nutshell. If you really want to play golf — the game as it should be played — the links of Scotland are the only place to be.

Take the Fear out of Sloping Lies

BY TONY JACKLIN

Tackling shots from sloping lies where the ball is above or below the feet or up or downhill seems to cause the handicap player a great deal of anguish.

It should not. For the shot from the situations where the ball is on other than a flat lie is no more difficult than the ordinary stroke; it just requires a little bit of adjustment and understanding of what is required to get the desired result.

I believe that many players just fill their heads with theoretical mumbo jumbo when faced with an uneven lie and then think their way to a bad shot.

The rules are quite simple and if observed there should be no need to fear the hilly lie at all. It is not a "bad" lie or a "difficult" lie it is just one of the many you will encounter in a round of golf and should be treated that way.

Much has been written on the subject already and I think many teachers have put uneven lies into the "difficult" category because they urge the player to adopt crazy postures in an attempt to iron out the slope. There is no need for that.

Your own body is perfectly capable of adapting to the requirement to stand to the ball and maintain balance without falling over. The idea that somehow you should adapt yourself to the shape of the slope by leaning in the general direction of it is, to my mind, just nonsense.

When you face a downhill or an uphill shot the only adaptation your body has to make is to flex the leg which is further up the slope to give you a solid stance.

After that it is a question of taking into account a slightly different swing arc and making sure that the ball position at address is correct.

On an uphill lie (for the right hander) the left leg will be slightly more flexed and the ball position will need to be slightly more forward i.e. further up the hill.

Because the ball will fly higher from this lie, select at least one club more than you would from the same distance on a flat lie and don't be afraid to take plenty of club. The arc of your swing will be slightly shorter, which is another reason for being generous in your club selection.

The essential thing on a sloping lie like this is to make a good clean contact with the ball and ball position is therefore vital to the whole

Continued on page 10

exercise.

Take a stance on the slope and have a practice swing. Watch for the point of contact with the turf and that will give you the guide to where to position the ball in relation to your stance.

From there it is simply a question of applying your normal swing and concentrating on making an accurate and clean contact with the ball.

When the ball is on a downslope the reverse of the above applies. Position the ball further back in the stance, but take at least one club less than you would from the same

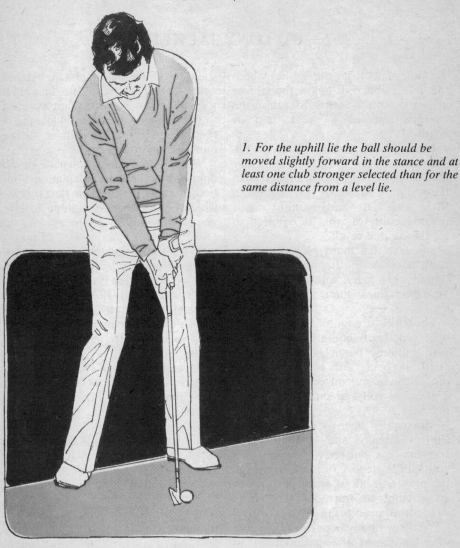

1. For the uphill lie the ball should be moved slightly forward in the stance and at least one club stronger selected than for the same distance from a level lie.

distance on a flat lie and again check the ball position at address with the aid of your practice swing.

Sidehill lies demand different adjustments, but again a ball that is above or below your feet shouldn't be any more difficult to strike accurately if you make the adjustments correctly.

With the ball above your feet the plane of your swing will be flatter and there will be a tendency to hook the ball off this kind of lie.

Stand a little further from the ball, again assessing just how much by taking a practice swing. The shot will

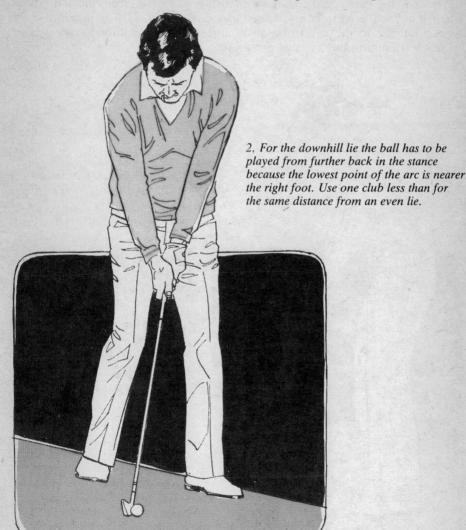

2. For the downhill lie the ball has to be played from further back in the stance because the lowest point of the arc is nearer the right foot. Use one club less than for the same distance from an even lie.

almost certainly come out a lower trajectory and have a tendency to be moving right to left (again for the right handed player) which means that very often less club is required than would be needed from the same distance off a flat lie.

It follows, of course, that the opposite is the case for the shot with the ball below the feet. You will need to stand closer to the ball to be able to reach it comfortably, so again use the practice swing to make the necessary adjustments.

From this position the plane of your swing will be more upright than normal with a shallower arc and it is a good idea to work on the basis that you will need one more club than usual to compensate. The ball will also tend to fade from this kind of lie so don't fight it, just make a slight adjustment in your aim to take care of it.

3. With the ball above the feet stand further back and take into account that the ball will finish left of the initial aiming point.

The same applies to the uphill lie. Simply bear in mind that the ball is likely to finish a bit left of where you initially aimed it and make allowances for that fact.

But the one essential thing above all else is not to worry about a lie that is not flat. It isn't more difficult, it's just different and a modified set of rules applies.

Learn the rules and make use of the evidence of your practice swing to make sure you get the ball in the correct position at address and then trust in your normal swing to get the job done.

Uneven lies are like every other shot in golf generally regarded as being difficult. The only fear is fear itself and that can be totally erased by understanding what is required to overcome a simple problem and then presenting a positive attitude and response to it.

4. For the shot with the ball below the feet it is necessary to stand closer to the ball to make a good, clean contact. Select one club more and make allowances for the shot finishing right of the initial aiming point.

THE NORTH

THE Highlands of Scotland to most people mean great mountains, majestic scenery, marvellous rivers to fish and an endless supply of single malt the more to savour the joys of this still largely unspoiled region of Britain.

But where the great mountains and glens relent towards the east side of the country nature left just enough ground for pursuants of the royal and ancient game to add another dimension to this great tourist attraction.

THE city of Perth has always been considered the gateway to the

Below — The Famous Gleneagles Hotel, Tayside. Right — Looking across the Queens Course at Gleneagles.

Highlands and so it is but for the golfer the Highlands as such has less significance than the North as a whole and a much more significant city in those terms perhaps is Aberdeen. A line drawn diagonally across the country between the two of them is as good a cut-off as any to consider the golf courses of the North.

Above that imaginary line lies the bulk of Scotland's acres but by comparison with the rest of the country far fewer of its golf courses.

The majority are spread out like a ribbon around the east coast from Aberdeen to the furthermost north club on mainland Scotland, Reay near Thurso, with its six short holes, a £4 green fee and grand views of the wild waters of the Pentland Firth.

But if the North lacks the concentration of courses of the central belt of Scotland it does not lack for quality for along that eastern shore are located courses acknowledged to be among the finest to be found anywhere.

IN 1780 a handful of gentlemen in the city of Aberdeen banded

together to found the Society of Golfers at Aberdeen, and the club which made much of its bicentenary celebrations seven years ago is now Royal Aberdeen and one of the oldest golf clubs in the world.

The original ballot box, used by the club to pass judgement on prospective members when the "black ball" system was still the rule of the day, still remains intact, if not in use, at the club today. It is preserved as a symbol of the history and traditions of this great club wherein it would be true to say the feminist movement are unlikely ever to hold an annual convention.

Ladies are welcome however on the course, in the dining room and the large lounge. Members of Aberdeen Ladies use the same course but they maintain a separate clubhouse.

Robert Simpson is credited with building Royal Aberdeen after it moved from its original seven-hole layout on the neighbouring King's Links to its present site at Balgownie across the River Don.

At just over 6400 yards it is a fine test of golf but prospective visitors should have a letter of introduction from their own club secretary and are advised to make arrangements in advance with the club.

SEPARATED from the delights of Royal Aberdeen by nothing more than a few simple stakes is the great links of Murcar designed by another Simpson, this time Archie, whose layout has stood the test of time well since it came into existence in 1909.

The 7th tee at Murcar commands one of the great views in golf with the crashing North Sea rollers on the right and a rolling strip of links between craggy outcrops on the left and the burn which meanders down the right

and also winds its way across the fairway.

To reach the safety of that fairway requires a carry from the tee not much short of 200 yards over the double loop of the burn and from there about the same again to reach the slightly raised green.

Club selection is difficult and reckoned always to be "one more" than first thought of and, if the pin is at the back, a couple more still if by which time you have any spare at all.

The same recommendation regarding a letter of introduction is just as valid at Murcar as at Royal Aberdeen, and it is worth remembering that Murcar has a little nine hole course which is ideal for the younger members of the family or as a warm-up for the main event.

THERE are many other courses in the Aberdeen area well worth a visit and perhaps none more so than the relatively new course at Westhill, located on the A944 about six miles from the city.

The course was built in 1977 and is relatively short at 5866 yards but it is perched high on a hill and seldom if ever is it free of a stiff breeze from one point of the compass or another. There are few more friendly places to pursue the royal and ancient game and visitors can play any day except a Saturday and there is a particularly warm welcome there for youngsters.

Westhill operates one of the most progressive youth policies anywhere in Britain and their example of how to encourage junior players is an example to everyone with the future of the game at heart.

SOME 22 miles north east of Aberdeen in a remote and beautiful spot nestling among great

Pitlochry Golf Club, Pitlochry, Tayside.

sand dunes is the famous links of Cruden Bay now perhaps rather less traditionally named the Cruden Bay Golf and Country Club.

It has its origins as far back as 1791 but has only been sited on its present position for less than 90 years of its long and illustrious history.

Former Ryder Cup player and master of the "suppressed six-iron", Harry Bannerman, is the professional at Cruden Bay where not so long ago the construction of an oil pipeline from the Forties Field in the North Sea threatened several of the holes. Fortunately the threat receded when wiser counsels prevailed in much the same way ironically as the price of the commodity itself has done as dramatically since. But if there is a wealth of fine courses around the Aberdeen area the traveller who heads north along the coast will find even more to tempt him to halt his journey.

If, however, he is intent only on the great and famous links then Nairn and the mystical Royal Dornoch will be set firmly in his sights.

ALONG with Royal Aberdeen, Cruden Bay and Murcar, Nairn and Dornoch complete what might be described as the "big five" of the mighty links of the North. To play them all is a tour de force which few who complete it will ever forget.

The least sung of the five is Nairn, a few miles from Inverness, and now more accessible since the completion of the new A9 trunk road, one of the spin-offs from the North Sea oil boom.

It is without doubt one of the most underrated of all our golf courses presenting a subtle but so difficult challenge. It starts with a solid par four of 400 yards along the beach and follows it immediately with a tough par five with a dry ditch which runs across the fairway.

Unlike the other courses in the group of five Nairn is not built among the sand dunes. It has been carved out among great stands of whin and masses of heather which threaten on most of the holes.

First laid out in 1887 it was modified and extended a couple of years later by Old Tom Morris who made the journey from St Andrews to do the job. Subsequent to that James Braid put his stamp on the course by way of refinement and that is the way it stands today.

It is famous, and rightly so, for the quality of its turf and the greens are fast and firm in the finest traditions of links golf. To nip an iron off the firm fairways of Nairn is one of the true delights of golf in Scotland and a sound reminder of the way things ought to be.

The 14th is perhaps the most memorable of the Nairn holes. It is a long par 3 of 206 yards played from the highest point on the course down to an undulating green with a backdrop of the Moray Firth and the Black Isle. On a sunny morning there are few finer views to be found anywhere the game of golf is played and a par figure there is a worthwhile achievement indeed.

To complete the nap hand of Scotland's northern courses requires little more than an hour's drive from Nairn. The fact that it is in the general direction of the Arctic Circle matters not a bit for the climate is much less severe than might be imagined and it is a shame that this majestic links has the reputation of being remote.

Certainly it requires some determination to get there but with improvements which have been made to the roads system it is not a trying journey at all and the rewards for the effort are immense.

ROYAL Dornoch has long been considered a pilgrimage for those with more than just a passing interest in the history and traditions of the game.

Ben Crenshaw and Tom Watson are among its greatest fans and Crenshaw particularly feels more for the place than most. He played there before a recent Open Championship and was so captivated by the mighty links that he was reported as not wanting to leave for the Championship. Without a doubt if it was located nearer the main centres of population in the south Dornoch would long since have been on the Open Championship rota.

But it has had recognition from golf headquarters at St Andrews just the same. In 1985 Royal Dornoch was the venue for the Amateur Championship and five years ealier it hosted the Home Internationals.

Royal Dornoch is an ancient links and appears in the very earliest records of the game in Scotland. Old Tom Morris was again a great influence in the layout of the course as the game became more organised but it is only in the past forty or so years that it reached its present form.

The legendary golf course architect, Donald Ross, was the little town's greatest "export" and other great names like Joyce and Roger Wethered have had long associations with the town and the course.

Tom Watson is on record as saying that at Dornoch he had more fun playing golf than aywhere else he has played. Those who make the effort to go there will undoubtedly feel the same.

A look at golf in the North would not however be complete without including Gleneagles. Strictly speaking

The scenic Boat of Garten in Highland Region.

it is only on the verge of the North by our declared rule of thumb but it is usually considered north by the majority who make their way to that most picturesque part of the country.

It is a golfing destination known the world over of course and may well rank second only to St Andrews as a mecca for visitors from across the Atlantic or Japan.

In 1980 the Gleneagles Hotel added to the Glendevon course to make a total of four courses in all on spectacular moorland site.

James Braid did the original design work on the King's and Queen's courses with a view to creating layouts for the enjoyment of the visitors to the splendid Gleneagles Hotel rather than strenuous examinations for the tournament player.

However, Gleneagles has had its fair share of important events including the Curtis Cup and the Penfold Tourn- ament in the mid 1930's as well as a match between the professionals of Britain and the United States in 1921 which was a forerunner of the Ryder Cup. The hotel was not then finished and recently discovered photographs taken at the event show the great shell of the hotel still awaiting completion and Jock Hutchison posing for the camera in front of the building on his birthday only a few weeks after he won the Open Championship at his native St Andrews.

The King's Course is the principal Gleneagles course and can be set up at more than 6800 yards for major events. The Queen's is shorter and the Prince's shorter still at just over 4600 yards. There is something to suit the standard for everybody who wants to play golf among some of Scotland's most spectacular scenery, and of course will not be found wanting when the plate is passed out for the green offering.

THE golfing visitor fond of a drop of Islay Malt can do a lot worse than combine his tastes very nicely at the Islay Golf Club at Machrie.

Thirty-five minutes by Loganair from Glasgow and the course lies as it was laid out in 1891 by Willie Campbell on the west side of the island along the shore of Laggan Bay and the crashing Atlantic.

The Machrie Hotel has several golf holiday packages to offer and it's well worth contacting them for details for once seen and played the urge to stay a little longer is hard indeed to resist.

ELSEWHERE in the west of Scotland there are dozens of courses which welcome visitors. Glasgow alone has twenty within the city boundary with the Glasgow Golf Club at Killermont one of the oldest clubs in the world.

This year it celebrates its bi-centenary and is considered to be the eighth oldest golf club in the world. The club has a second course Glasgow Gailes which is 35 miles away and adjoins Western Gailes.

Visitors will find it easier to play at Glasgow Gailes than Killermont where visitors are not generally encouraged but contact with the secretary might prove fruitful and if permission is granted then the rewards are well worth the effort.

Haggs Castle, venue for the new Scottish Open on the P.G.A. European Tour last year is literally at the end of the urban motorway in Glasgow and as such must just be about the most accessible course in the west of Scotland. It is a pleasant parkland layout but again it is a private club and permission to play has to be sought from the secretary.

ELSEWHERE in and around the city there are many courses which welcome visitors and on a wider front there are some thirty municipal courses in Strathclyde as a whole. There are for instance the Darley and Lochgreen courses at Troon which are good enough to have been pressed into service as Open Championship qualifying courses and only Bellisle at Ayr is a serious challenger as far as severity is concerned although it is a parkland course and totally different from the links of Troon.

THERE are courses from Bogside to Wishaw and virtually all the letters of the alphabet in between in this golf rich region and if the visitor moves a little further south there is the majesty of Southerness to add as well.

Southerness probably ranks as one of the great "unknown" courses but is fast becoming less so as word gets out about this relative newcomer, which is almost as remote as Dornoch. Mackenzie Ross who rebuilt Turnberry after the war was brought in to design Southerness which opened for play in 1947.

What he created was a monster which required in more recent time a little taming and today is a severe test over its 6548 yards from the medal tees. It can be stretched to 7000 yards if needs be but brave would be the player who tackled that assault from choice.

Long carries from the tee, tight fairways and tough rough are the order of the day at Southerness and if the visitor has a mind to play that kind of golf and find out how well he is equipped to tackle it then it's the place to go. It's one of very few genuine links courses built since the last War and it was venue for the Scottish Amateur Championship in 1985.

THE EAST

THE east of Scotland, and particularly the east coast of Scotland, is the traditional home of the royal and ancient game. It was on the linksland along the coast that the game became established on ground eminently suited to the purpose.

Waste ground, which nature had reclaimed from the sea over the centuries, was little use for anything other than leisure activities and so the first golf courses emerged among the sand dunes and the gorse and broom bushes.

From Edinburgh to St Andrews there is a veritable Aladdin's Cave of courses which the visitor could spend many months exploring without running out of new challenges to play.

One of the original clubs was founded at Leith by the Gentlemen Golfers of Edinburgh, now of course known the world over as the

Craigmiller Golf Course, Edinburgh.

Honorable Company of Edinburgh Golfers.

The club was formed in 1744 and Duncan Forbes of Culloden, who became famous as the man who tried to put down the uprising of the Clans the following year, was their first President.

For the first 45 years of the club's existence the members played over five holes at Leith before moving to Gullane just along the coast. There today stands the great links of Muirfield which rates among the very finest courses to be found anywhere the game is played.

Many sons of the members of the club went to the University of St Andrews to complete their education and just over a decade after the Honourable Company was formed a group of gentlemen and noblemen formed the Society of St Andrews Golfers, which today is known as the Royal and Ancient Golf Club of St Andrews, the governing body for the game and, together with the United States Golf Association, makers and arbiters on the rules of golf.

Between these two clubs is stretched out the heartland of golf in Scotland and the two courses over which these two clubs play is an appropriate point to start a look at golf in the east coast.

ALTHOUGH they have so much in common in terms of their contribution to the game the courses over which they play could hardly be more different. St Andrews is known the world over as the Home of Golf and rightly so for its links have echoed to the sound of club on ball for centuries.

It has been, and unless some great catastrophe dictates otherwise, always will remain a public links. The Royal and Ancient Club, with its famous and imposing clubhouse immediately behind the first tee and beside the equally famous 18th green, does not own the golf course over which its members play. It shares with several other clubs in the town certain privileges but the Old Course is run by the Links Management Committee for the benefit of the golfing public as a whole and anyone with the wherewithall to meet the green offering can go to pay homage to the Old Lady of St Andrews.

For most of the year a ballot system operates and those wishing to pit their wits against the Old Course first have to battle their way through that. It is quite simply done. Names placed with the starter the day before the players wish to play are entered in the ballot and the lucky ones drawn out get a tee time for the following day.

To play there is to experience one of the great delights the game of golf has to offer. No-one is sure how old the Old Course is although it is certain that it dates back to the 15th century. In the last 150 years it has changed little, indeed it is said that the last change made to the Old Lady was the removal of the bunker on the first fairway, and that removal work was carried out around the time the Titanic was making her ill-fated maiden voyage.

THE Old Course has a unique atmosphere which Ben Crenshaw once described as like "walking with the ghosts of the past." There is no other golf course like it in the world with its big double greens, wide fairways and bunkers within which it is at times on the one hand difficult to stand, and at others as easy to get lost.

It also has arguably the most famous hole in golf — the 17th or Road Hole.

The Road Hole has been a graveyard for many championship hopes over the years, none more so in recent times than poor Tommy Nakajima of Japan who, when in a strong position to win the Open Championship in 1978 took nine strokes for the hole, the vast majority of them in the Road Hole bunker which eats into the heart of the green. Inevitably the bunker has become known as the "Sands of Nakajima" and while the likeable Japanese has been the most notable of its more modern victims many, many have fallen at the Road Hole before him.

However, the Old Course is not the only St Andrews course and visitors unsuccessful in the ballot, or who prefer their golf at a slightly faster pace, have the choice of three other fine courses.

THE New Course is by far the toughest test and many feel it is more difficult in some ways than the Old Course which is played by visitors, from more forward tees and to slightly easier pin placements.

The Eden Course on the west side of the Old Course is a delightful eighteen holes with many fine holes and is a fine test of golf despite not being over long.

Each year St Andrews holds the Eden Tournament which is open to visitors and features qualifying rounds on both the Eden and the New courses. Thereafter there is matchplay for those successful in the qualifying and supplementary events for those who are not, all of which adds up to a great week of golf and highly recommended for the travelling golfer who intends to spend a week at the Home of Golf.

Soon a new course is to be opened at St Andrews and it surely is destined to be one of Scotland's greatest courses. It will be an amalgam of the Jubilee Course, fourth St Andrews course, and the New Course and plans are already well advanced. It will be a genuine alternative to the Old Course itself when the plan reaches fruition.

Unlike the Old Course at St Andrews, however, the famous links of Muirfield is far from being a public place. Indeed it is probably the least public of all the Scottish courses and to play there is to have either enjoyed the invitation of a member of the Honorable Company or to have been successful in negotiations with the club secretary some time in advance.

For those who succeed by either method the rewards are immeasurable but there are rules to be observed and short shrift for those who don't abide by them.

AT Muirfield foursomes is still the accepted form of the game and three hours is far too long to be going

Left — The Silver Clubs in The Royal & Ancient Golf Club, St. Andrews, Fife.

about it. At Muirfield the buffet has no pier save perhaps at Old Prestwick or Bruntsfield and the game is still played on traditional links turf where pop-up sprinklers are neither contemplated nor required and "preferred lies" are a relative form of perjury and nothing to do with fairways.

Visitors with an interest in the history of the game might like to stop at Musselburgh where golf is known to have been played in 1672 and it is likely that it was played there long before that too.

It may well have been the first place that golf was played on what we today would consider to be a "proper" course and although today it does not hold the position in the game that it once did there is much of the history of the game there. The Championship was held there in 1874 when the biggest field thus far assembled for the event gathered — a total of 32 players.

Mungo Park of Musselburgh won on his home course and The Open was to be held there a further five times up till 1889 when Willie Park Jnr, also of Musselburgh, won with a total of 155 and after a tie with the great Andrew Kirkcaldy.

Close by Muirfield is the small town of Gullane which is steeped in the royal and ancient game and claims four courses, three of which are conveniently numbered in rotation from one through three while the fourth is known as Luffness New, despite the fact that it is not new at all having been established in 1894.

A letter of introduction to the secretary at Luffness New is advisable for the casual visitor, and better still is to make contact in advance to make

Left — Dollar Golf Course, Central Region.

arrangements to play. There are no restrictions on the "numbered" courses the most famous of which is the No 1 course which has many times been a qualifying course for the Open Championship. The other courses are slightly shorter but nonetheless interesting for that and to play any of them is to breathe the atmosphere of the ancient game in very much its original surroundings.

Further down the coast the courses at North Berwick and Dunbar beckon the visitor and offer great traditional golf.

The North Berwick Golf Club is one of the most venerable in Scotland and boasts former Prime Minister, Lord Balfour, among its past captains. The club was formed in 1832 and it retains the concept of the game of that period.

Walls have to be carried on occasions from the tee and it is not unusual at all to have to carry large segments of the North Sea to seek a safe haven from which to play your next.

DUNBAR is another of Scotland's famous courses and is one of fewer than a dozen formed before 1800. The official date is 1794 and since then many have tried but few have succeeded in taming this magnificent narrow strip of traditional links where the wind howls in from the North Sea and the test is as much of character as of prowess.

In Edinburgh itself there are many fine courses such as Bruntsfield, Royal Burgess, Ratho Park and Dalmahoy all of which allow visitors.

The Royal Burgess Golfing Society of Edinburgh stakes its own claim to be the oldest golf club in the world and has written evidence of its existence since April the 8th, 1773. It was known to be in existence before that and on the basis that 1735 was the actual date, the Society held its 250th anniversary celebrations in 1985 and right royally at that.

Bruntsfield is another of the oldest clubs in the world dating back to 1761 and commands wonderful views of the Firth of Forth from its parkland layout at the west end of the city.

Ratho Park is another enjoyable parkland course well worth a visit and Dalmahoy Golf and Country Club has a fine course which has hosted many important events on both the amateur and professional calendars.

From there it is a short trip across the Forth Road Bridge to the ancient Kingdom of Fife where pursuit of the royal and ancient game is conducted with an intensity equalled in very few places the game is played. And rightly so for the Kingdom has a magnificent offering of courses to lay before the traveller on his way to St Andrews.

There is the beautiful parkland course of the Dunfermline Golf Club at Pitfirrane House at Crossford with its ancient clubhouse and fine layout. A letter of introduction or prior arrangement is the order of the day there but well worth the effort. Just

Musselburgh Old Course one of Scotland's earliest courses, Lothian Region.

along the way at Burntisland there is no requirement for either and visitors can play without restriction.

THE Burntisland club with its magnificent views over the Forth to Edinburgh on the far shore is not long — well under 6000 yards — but it is tight and testing and ideal for honing the game for the assualt on the big links further up the coast.

A stop at Ladybank on the way will refine the process even more for this excellent heathland course is an Open Championship qualifying test and one of the best of its kind anywhere.

Tight fairways, deep gorse and impenetrable heather are the hallmarks of Ladybank, no doubt apocryphal, of the player who went deep into the player who went deep into the Ladybank rough in search of his ball and was gone for some time.

His playing partners conscious of the time being spent in the search urged their companion to give up the cause since seldom if ever had a ball been found that deep in the Ladybank rough. "I'm not looking for the ball," came the reply from deep in the jungle, "I'm looking for my clubs!" Keep the ball in play or take plenty of golf balls is sound advice for those who would pit their skills against this excellent course.

On a line almost due east from Ladybank lies, on the coast, one end of a string of majestic golf courses strung out like a priceless necklace along the shores of the Firth of Forth with the other end at the Home of Golf itself on St Andrews Bay.

The first is the old links of Leven, truly one of Scotland's great golf courses. Two clubs share this ancient links, Leven Golfing Society and Leven Thistle Golf Club.

Like St Andrews, Leven is a public

links and nowadays a starting time system operates and like its next door neighbour, Lundin Links, Leven is an Open Championship qualifying course. The Innerleven Club from which Leven Golfing Society was formed was one of the dozen or so oldest golf clubs in the world and the course preserves all the qualities of traditional links golf.

THE 18th hole is one of the finest finishing holes to be found anywhere. A long par four it is played normally into the prevailing wind and requires a long carry over the Scoonie Burn which twists its way round the front of the green in front of the Society's clubhouse.

Next door Lundin Links is a private club but welcomes visitors. In years gone by the holes on the south side of the now non-existent railway line were combined with the similarly sited holes on the Leven course to form the original Leven course which was nine out and nine back.

Today the holes on the north side of the old railway line at Lundin Links are more inland in character than their equivalent at Leven but command more spectacular views over the Firth of Forth.

Muirfield can be seen on a clear day from the 13th fairway at Lundin Links and the 14th hole, a spectacular downhill par three over gorse with out of bounds over the wall on to the Leven course on the right, is aptly named "Perfection".

Along the coast a few miles the fine links of Elie makes yet another contrast in style. It is more undulating, immaculately kept, as indeed are its neighbours, but is unique in the fact that the starter used a periscope salvaged from a submarine to monitor play from the first tee. The drive is blind over the hill and the command to "play away please" is called only after "up periscope."

FOR those who like something a little different there is an interesting little nine hole course at Anstruther, the old fishing village in the East Neuk of Fife.

It is perched on top of the headland and while it is unlikely to go on the rota of Open Championship courses even if the R & A relent in their determination to always hold the Championship on an eighteen hole course, it is still worth a visit.

From there the road leads to the ancient burgh of Crail, the last stop before St Andrews and home to another of the game's oldest courses.

Crail Golfing Society dates back to 1786 and although it is only a few yards over 5700 when the wind whistles off the sea around Fifeness as it usually does it is one of the toughest tests under 6000 yards to be found anywhere. Balcomie Links has a magic about it which only those who have ever played it can appreciate and in fine weather it is nothing short of idyllic.

There are few more friendly places to play and visitors will find the greens small and difficult to hit but always marvellous to putt upon once you are there.

It is a fitting place from which to mount the final assault on St Andrews itself still the ultimate aspiration for the vast majority who come to Scotland to pursue the royal and ancient game.

There, no doubt, eternal peace will be found for some when the goal is reached, but forget not the journey for along it lies a golfing challenge and a welcome unequalled anywhere in the world

THE WEST AND SOUTH

hole course at Lochgilphead in Argyll and Bute District once described so eloquently by S.L. McKinlay as "almost an act of faith rather than an exercise in the most agreeable and exacting of pastimes".

TURNBERRY is the one which perhaps springs most easily to mind following Greg Norman's victory in the 1986 Open Championship. It is one of golf's greatest links and of course was the venue for the epic battle between Jack Nicklaus and Tom Watson in 1977 which produced one of the best finishes ever seen in the history of the Championship.

Last year Norman battled against the elements and a golf course with fearsome rough and narrow fairways to beat off the challenge of the best players in the world. In the process he equalled the nominal par of the Ailsa Course which is 70. Visitors to Turnberry have to part with quite a handful of coin of the realm for the privilege of playing this great championship course but few indeed are those who deem afterwards that it was not worth it.

TURNBERRY also has the Arran course which has to play second fiddle to its more famous neighbour but do not let the fact that it is the second string fool you. It is a great course in its own right and with special terms for playing it rather than the championship course it's a very good alternative.

A little known alternative to the Turnberry courses for the visitor in that particular corner of Ayrshire is the pleasant holiday course at Girvan which has eight holes neatly strung along the shore with the remainder across the road, and of an inland nature.

THE vast Region of Strathclyde on the west side of Scotland has somewhere in the region of 150 of Scotland's golf courses within its borders and for our rough rule of thumb split of the country is represents virtually the whole of the area we consider The West and South.

It stretches as far north as Oban, which strictly speaking is into the Highlands and has an 18 hole course which requires no introduction and imposes no restrictions on anyone except on the days when there is a club competition. But the majority of the courses are grouped around the industrial centre of Glasgow with the West's great championship links strung southwards down the Ayrshire coast.

The range of courses available to the visitor is wide indeed from the most fearsome of the mighty championships links like the 1986 Open Championship venue at Turnberry to the little nine

By Turnberry standards it is a lot shorter but the views, particularly on the links holes, are just as spectacular over the Firth as they are six miles down the road.

The west of Scotland is of course associated principally with its championship links, Turnberry being one of a group of three close together on the lovely Ayrshire coast.

THE most historic is Prestwick, where the first Open Championship was held in 1860 and won by Willie Park of Musselburgh with a score of 174. The field for that inaugural event was eight players, as indeed it was the following year at the same venue when Old Tom Morris of the home club won the first of his four Championship Belts.

Prestwick is as historic as St Andrews

and the ghosts of the past still tread this rough and ready links in the same way that they do at the Home of Golf.

Originally it was twelve holes and for the Championship the players played three rounds in the one day over the 3799 yards it measured then.

In 1851 the Prestwick Golf Club was formed and today its clubhouse is one of the great golfing institutions. To take lunch at the long table at Prestwick is an experience long to be remembered and cherished for there are few to match it anywhere the game is played.

The course today is of eighteen holes and this year it will host the Amateur Championship, the first time since 1952 when Harvey Ward of the United States defeated his fellow countryman Frank Stranahan by six and five in the final.

Prestwick hosted the first twelve

Turnberry course and Hotel Strathclyde Region.

The Turnberry Lighthouse and Ailsa Craig from the 9th at Turnberry.

Open Championships, eight of which were won by Old and Young Tom Morris between them, before it gave up the sole rights and the championship moved to St Andrews for the first time in 1873.

Jim Barnes of the United States was the last winner of an Open Championship at Prestwick in 1925, since when it has been off the Open rota because of the difficulties of accommodating spectators.

Prestwick boasts one of the most terrifying opening holes in golf. It is a mere 346 yards in length but all the way down the right side of the fairway runs a wall which separates the course from the railway and the out of bounds. On the left is deep rough and the prevailing wind will normally be over the player's left shoulder with the result that British Rail Prestwick has probably as good a stock of new golf balls as the very personable Frank Rennie has in the club's professional's shop.

Prestwick is most easily identified by the great Cardinal bunkers which cross the fairway at the third and are the subject of many of the famous illustrations of the course from the past. It used to be, in the days of less efficient equipment than we have

today, that two good shots were required to carry the Cardinal bunkers but today with modern balls and clubs the 482 yards of the par five third hole can be reached by the longer hitters in two shots — if the wind is right of course.

If you play it savour it and take the time to have a look around the clubhouse carefully too for there is much in the way of the history of the game there for the interested observer.

THE third of the great championship links along that beautiful part of the Ayrshire coast is Royal Troon, only a short distance from the original home of the Open Championship.

It was first used as an Open venue in 1923 when Arthur Havers took the title of Champion Golfer for the year. He was the last Englishman to win until the legendary Henry Cotton eleven years later.

Three names stick out in recent memory at this famous links. The first is Gene Sarazen who failed to qualify when Arthur Havers won in 1923 and then came back to Troon in 1973 to hole his tee shot at the famous Postage Stamp with a five-iron. It was a stroke seen around the world and a wonderfully sentimental return for Sarazen, then into his seventies.

Arnold Palmer came to Troon in

1962 as the current Open Champion having won the previous year at Royal Birkdale. The course was hard and running very difficult but rather like Greg Norman last year at Turnberry Palmer mastered the conditions and won by six strokes, the biggest margin of modern times. Centenary Open Champion Kel Nagle was second but there was no-one else nearer to Palmer than thirteen strokes.

In 1982, the last time the Open was held at Troon a young man called Bobby Clampett set the golfing world on its head when he opened with rounds of 67 and 66 and looked certain to be an all-the-way winner. But the young man, who is a product of a method of teaching golf known as "The Golfing Machine" pioneered by the late Homer Kelley, added rounds of 78 and 77 to his openers and slipped ingloriously out of a Championship it seemed impossible for him to lose.

But Troon like St Andrews in that respect has a nasty habit of sneaking up on the player just when he thinks he is home and dry. There are many memorable holes on this mighty links but perhaps the most famous is the short 8th known as "The Postage Stamp". It only measures about 120 yards from the tees which the visitor plays but depending on the wind it can play as long as a No 3 or No 4 iron or the merest breath with a wedge.

The green is devilishly difficult to hit and hold and to miss it on the right and get in one of the greenside bunkers there can mean a protracted spell with the sand iron.

The 11th with the railway running all the way down the right side of the fairway is another of the famous Troon holes where, from the championship tee, is almost impossible to see any safe haven for the tee shot. A strong nerve indeed is required to launch a drive out over the acres of gorse confronting those on that tee and only the most soundly struck drive sufficient for well over a 200 yard carry will suffice.

Tom Weiskopf won his one Open title there in 1973 and Tom Watson the fourth of his five titles.

Book a time in advance if you want to play Royal Troon and take a letter of introduction from your club secretary, as well as a certificate of your handicap. The effort is worth it but remember that juniors are not allowed to play and ladies are restricted to Mondays, Wednesdays and Fridays and there are restrictions on ladies in the clubhouse, so check the current situation before playing.

FOR those who are quite happy to leave the big-named courses to others there is plenty of great golf to be found within a few miles of any of these great championship courses. Places like Western Gailes, a qualifying course for the Open Championship last year, and Glasgow Gailes spring immediately to mind and there is a fine course at Barassie which is more correctly called Kilmarnock Barassie very close to Royal Troon.

Professional there is Billy Lockie, a stalwart of the Scottish Tartan Tour and one of the nicest fellows playing the game anywhere. Prospective visitors should consult him for details but bear in mind that visitors to Barassie on Wednesdays and at weekends require to play with a member. All is well for the visitor for the rest of the week and juniors and ladies are welcome within specific times.

LOOKING out across the Firth of Clyde from any of these fine

Ayrshire courses already mentioned the view is dominated by the great lump of granite known as the Ailsa Craig and the often dark and mystical prospect of the Island of Arran. With its highest peak, Goat Fell, very often clothed in cloud the starkly beautiful island of Arran has also something to tempt the golfing traveller. It has, unusually these days and like Prestwick of old, a twelve hole course at Blackwaterfoot with a par of 41, a nine-hole layout at Corrie and eighteen holes at Brodick where the ferry from the mainland docks, and one or two others dotted around the island.

BACK on the mainland there is a whole gaggle of fine links from Ayr in the south to Wemyss Bay further up the coast and there are some of the most breathtaking views to be seen on a golf course anywhere from the fairways of the likes of Gourock, Millport, Largs Routenburn where Bob Torrance famous father of a famous son, is the resident pro, and Rothesay.

THERE are a handful of municipal courses in the Glasgow area all with something different to offer.

Littlehill on the north side of the city at Auchinairn could in other circumstances be an outstanding course but even allowing for the constraints of public ownership it is a fine test and many a golfstruck youngster has taken his first swing or two on its rolling fairways. It is perhaps the best of the municipal courses most of which are eminently playable while others would make no claim to challenge Augusta National as an alternative Masters venue. But they all provide a much needed outlet for those learning to play the game or who want simply to blow off golfing steam and more importantly

perhaps, a place for youngsters to play when such provisions are limited indeed.

THERE are two special courses on the west side of the country which demand special attention. Machrihanish is on the Kintyre peninsula and Machrie in Islay. Both lie exposed to the Atlantic Ocean and both offer a very special version of the royal and ancient game.

Like Royal Dornoch, Machrihanish is a famous but somewhat remote golf course for the visitor. To get there means some degree of effort if transport is by road but the course can be reached from Glasgow in little more than half an hour if the starting point is the airport.

The first nine holes at Machrihanish stand comparison with anything the game has to offer anywhere and the first of them is widely regarded as the toughest opening hole in Scotland.

It demands a carry of upwards of 200 yards to hit the perfect line and open up the possibility of hitting this long 400 yard hole in two shots. The Atlantic piles in on the left hand side and the hole moves from right to left to force a tee shot much in similar vein to the famous 9th at Turnberry from the championship tee.

Old Tom Morris made some changes to the course after it had been opened as a ten-hole layout and the great J.H. Taylor was brought in to update things to take account of new equipment in 1914. The job he did then remains virtually unchanged since nor is there any reason to even consider that it should. Machrihanish is a jewel in the west of Scotland's golfing crown and the great thing about it too is that it is very far from being overplayed.

THE BORDERS, LOTHIAN, AND FIFE

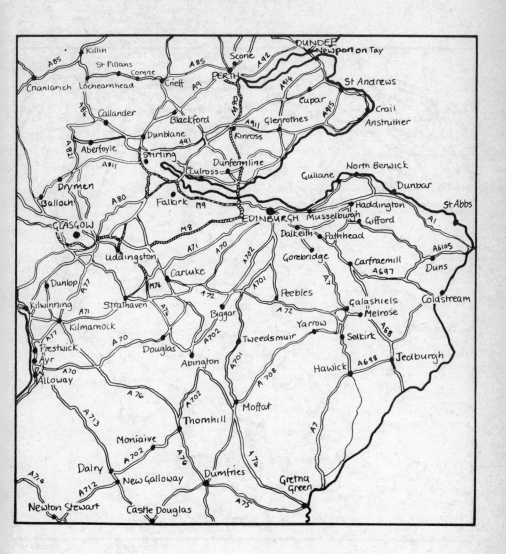

PERTH, ANGUS, ABERDEEN N.E.

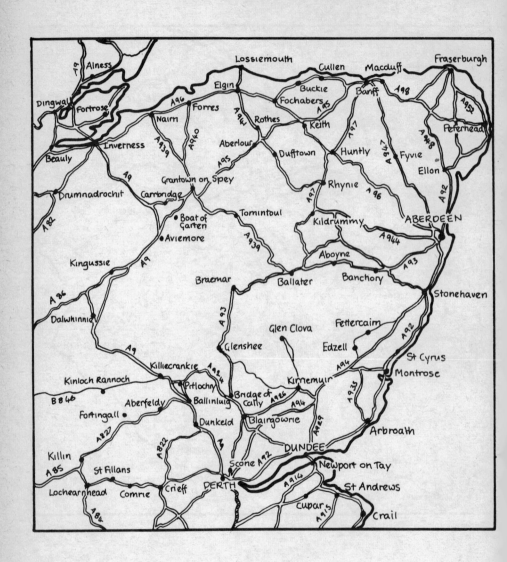

THE NORTHERN HIGHLANDS

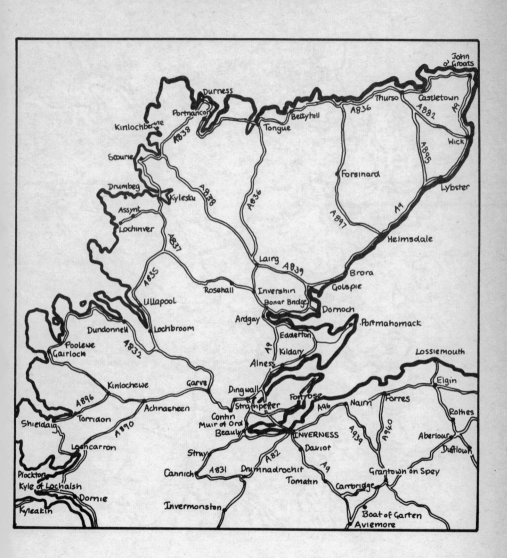

WESTERN AND CENTRAL
HIGHLANDS

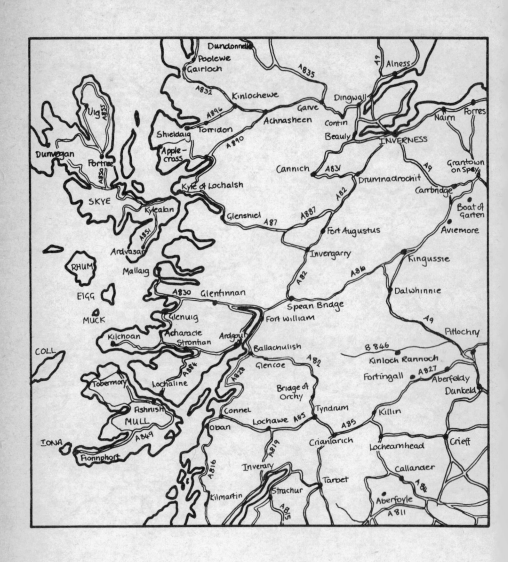

CENTRAL AND S.W.
SCOTLAND

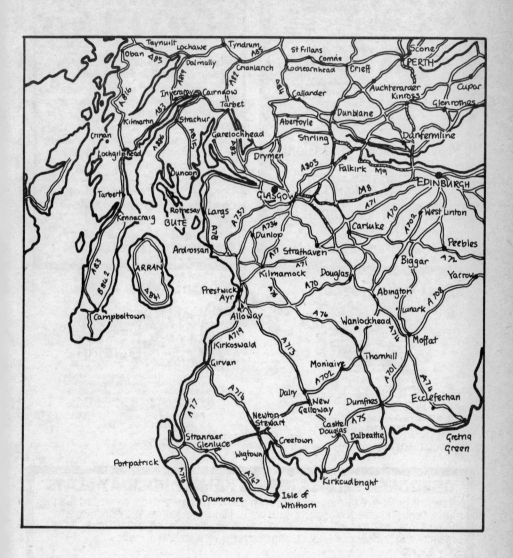

A
B
E
R
D
E
E
N
S
H
I
R
E

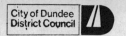

City of Dundee
District Council

Dundee is one stroke ahead when it comes to municipal golf facilities. A range of well kept and well designed courses cater for the serious and light-hearted, expert and beginner.

Within a 395 acre estate, there is a picturesque 18 hole S.S.S. 72 Championship golf course at Camperdown Park and at Caird Park there is an 18 hole S.S.S. 70 course, together with 2, par 3, 9 hole golf courses.

For further details relative to the booking system, green fees etc., contact the Leisure & Recreation Department, 353 Clepington Road, Dundee, telephone no. 0382 23141 Ext. 4413.

TURN TO PAGE 134
TO FIND THE A.A. MILEAGE CHART

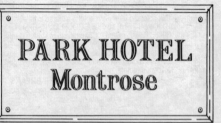

50

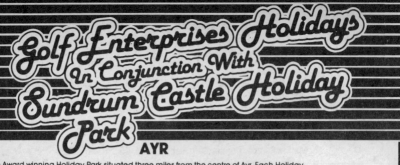

CHAPLE PARK HOUSE

Situated in the residential district of Ayr. 2 mins drive from Belleisle golf course, within easy reach of Royal Troon, Turnberry and Old Prestwick. All bedrooms have coloured TV, and tea making facilities. Open all year. Rates per person per day, Bed and Breakfast from £12 inc. VAT. For details write or phone: **Mrs. J. Gardner, Chaple Park House, 16 Ewenfield Road, Ayr. Tel: (0292) 262065.**

Recommended for golfers ...

ABBOTSFORD HOTEL
"Golfing in Ayrshire Open Golf Country"

Golf parties specifically catered for, in the olde worlde atmosphere of this elegant hotel, with bedrooms with en suite facilities, excellent food & beer garden. Special golf party rates, all tee bookings attended to. For further details contact Allan Hunter.

**Abbotsford Hotel,
Corsehill Road,
Ayr.
Tel: (0292) 261506**

54

BANFFSHIRE

CAITHNESS

Please mention this Pastime Publications guide.

60

Please mention this Pastime Publications guide.

64

66

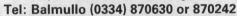

TURN TO PAGE 134
TO FIND THE A.A. MILEAGE CHART

KIRKCUDBRIGHTSHIRE

LANARKSHIRE

LOTHIAN

Redheugh Hotel

BAYSWELL PARK ● DUNBAR
Telephone: 0368 62793

Scottish Tourist Board
COMMENDED

Situated on the Firth of Forth, in good golfing country, we have 9 golf courses nearby, 2 being in Dunbar itself. We can offer a package with free golf. Enquiries welcome.
Our licensed, family-run hotel has recently been completely refurbished. All our bedrooms have central heating, colour television, radio, direct-dial telephone, tea/coffee-making facilities and private bathroom complete with shower.
Edinburgh, Scotland's fine capital, is only 45 mins. by road or 25 mins. by rail. The Redheugh, therefore, is suited both to the tourist and the business person.
Relax with a quiet drink in our residents' lounge while we prepare your meal, chosen from our exciting menus.
A warm welcome awaits you from Frank and Anne Creedican.

BELLEVUE HOTEL
DUNBAR

An elegant late Victorian Hotel, refurbished to a high standard, overlooking sea and East Links Championship Golf Course with inclusive Golf Breaks available throughout the year.
Gullane, North Berwick and other good Courses nearby.
Excellent restaurant and bar with real ale and malts.
Three day Golf Breaks from around £130 inclusive of Dinner and Green Fees.
Colour Brochure 0368 62322.

A PASTIME PUBLICATION
will help you
to find a Happy Holiday for all

SCOTLAND HOME OF GOLF

SCOTLAND FOR FISHING

SCOTLAND FOR THE MOTORIST

See our Guides on Sale
at Your Local Newsagent
and Book Shop.

PASTIME PUBLICATIONS
LIMITED

L O T H I A N

78

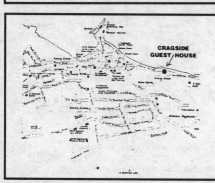

LOTHIAN

MORAYSHIRE

MORAYSHIRE

NAIRNSHIRE

PERTHSHIRE

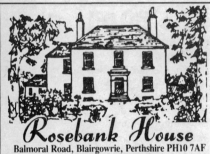

TURN TO PAGE 101 TO FIND GOLF COURSES AND CLUBS THROUGHOUT SCOTLAND

LOCKES ACRE HOTEL

Small very comfortable fully licensed family run hotel. Magnificent views overlooking McCrosty park and mountains beyond. Colour TV and tea and coffee making facilities in all rooms. Noted for excellent home cooking and baking. Within easy access of numerous 18 and 9 hole golf courses.
RAC ** STB 3 Crowns Commended. Excellent hygiene award.
For brochure please contact: Lockes Acre Hotel, Comrie Road, Crieff, Perthshire. Tel: (0764) 2526.

COACHMAN'S HOUSE

Beautiful modernised coach house in delightful rural setting, ½mile from Dunning, 10 miles west of Perth.
Accommodation for 8 provides linen, towels, colour T.V., washing & drying facilities. Cooking and water heating by Aga cooker.
9-hole golf course at Dunning. Gleneagles hotel golf courses 7 miles. Wet weather games facilities in our chapel.
Similar accommodation in Gean Tree Cottage — sleeps 4.
Ideal touring, golf and walking centre.
Ask for brochure:
**Mrs J. R. MARSHALL, Dalrioch, Dunning, Perth PH2 0QJ
Telephone (076484) 368**

LAVENDER COTTAGE

"Colliston", Glenfarg, Perth PH2 9PE

Pretty cottage situated half mile from Glenfarg amid superb countryside on quiet road. Ideally placed for touring, with Edinburgh, Dundee and St. Andrews within 30 miles; 30 miles from Perth. Enclosed garden; 2 bedrooms; living room; kitchen; bathroom; storage heaters. Open fire and colour TV.

Many famous golf courses nearby, including Gleneagles, St. Andrews, Rosemount, Carnoustie. Also available nearby — gliding, swimming, riding, fishing and hillwalking.
For further details contact **Mrs. J. Baillie or tel: (05773) 434**

THE ANGLER'S REST INN

Guildtown, Perthshire.
Tel: Balbeggie 329.

This old coaching Inn located 5¼ miles north of Perth on the A93, is noted for good cuisine and comfortable accommodation. Ideally sited for touring the central belt of Scotland. Fishing and golf facilities locally. Parking for 30 cars. Open all year under the supervision of the resident proprietor

Please mention this Pastime Publications guide.

PERTHSHIRE

DRUMMOND ARMS HOTEL
St. Fillans, Perthshire PH6 2NF
Set in the heart of the central Highlands on the shores of
beautiful LOCH EARN, The Drummond Arms provides the
ideal base from which to play any or all of the excellent golf
courses in the area including Gleneagles, St. Andrews and
St. Fillans own 9 hole course.
Tariff details:
April, May, June & Oct. £27.50 per person per night, Dinner,
Bed & Breakfast inclusive of golf. Minimum stay 3 nights. July, August & Sept. £30.00 per person per night,
Dinner Bed & Breakfast inclusive of golf. Minimum stay 3 nights. For further information write or telephone
to Euan Marshall, St. Fillans (076485) 212.

Ballathie House Hotel
A Privately Owned Country House Hotel of Distinction

Superbly located within its own estate 12 miles to the north of
Perth in an idyllic setting on the banks of the River Tay.

The nearby A9 and A93 bring a number of golf courses within easy
reach including Rosemount (10 mins), Gleneagles (35 mins),
Carnoustie and St. Andrews (50 mins).

22 rooms in the main Baronial Style House and 12 in the adjacent
Sportsman's Lodge all offer a high degree of comfort, private
bathroom, radio, TV and direct dial telephone. Ballathie is famous for
its cuisine — fresh local produce is cooked with care and imagination
— and our staff are attentive and friendly.

Send for comprehensive brochure and details of a wide range of
tariffs which offer flexibility to suit most budgets.

Kinclaven, by Stanley, Perthshire, PH1 4QN.
Tel: (025 083) 268

TO ASSIST WITH YOUR BOOKINGS
OR ENQUIRIES
YOU WILL FIND IT HELPFUL TO MENTION THIS
Pastime Publications Guide.

90

ROSS-SHIRE

Craigdarroch Lodge hotel

Ashley Courtenay, Egon Ronay and AA ★★ Recommended

Craigdarroch Lodge is a family run 2 Star Country House Hotel set in 12 acres of relaxing natural gardens and woodlands well known for its friendly atmosphere and log fires. There is a personal welcome awaiting you, and all that's best in Scottish cuisine and comfort. There are facilities for the young to the old which include tennis, grass bowls, full sized snooker table, salmon and trout fishing on our own beats.

Craigdarroch is the linkpin of Ross-shire for day trips to Wester-Ross, Sutherland, The Isle of Skye, Western Isles, Dornoch Firth, Black Isle, Inverness, Loch Ness and Moray Firth. Do not hesitate to ask for further information on our special interest package holidays, assistance in travel arrangements, and in house car hire facility.

Open all year round for residents and non residents, bar lunches and evening dinner.

CRAIGDARROCH LODGE HOTEL, Craigdarroch Drive, Contin, Ross-shire. Tel: Strathpeffer (0997) 21265.

TRADES DESCRIPTION ACT

The accommodation mentioned in this holiday guide has not been inspected, and the publishers rely on information provided. The publishers have every confidence in their advertisers but cannot be held responsible for the accuracy of the descriptions published.

Royal Hotel

Cathedral Square, Fortrose, Ross-shire IV10 8SU.

Situated half a mile from Fortrose and Rosemarkie Golf Club, the Royal is also within motoring time of Muir of Ord, Strathpeffer, Tain, Royal Dornoch and Nairn courses.

We offer comfortable accommodation and excellent food in pleasant surroundings. Special weekly golfing terms available.

For further information:
**Mr. Alastair Brown,
Royal Hotel,
Fortrose, Ross-shire.
Tel: (0381) 20236**

STITLINGSHIRE SUTHERLAND

WIGTOWNSHIRE

The Isle of Arran

Scotland in miniature

Sub-tropical palms grow in the open and pay tribute to the Gulf Stream's warm caress. Red deer roam, the golden eagle soars over the purple heather and the grey seal slips from grey rock.

There is so much to see and do for the lover of peace and beauty, the sportsman, the family, that the only problem is where to start.

Savour the Arran experience. Sail for an hour from busy, hustling West Central Scotland — and enter another world. Let the magic of the beautiful Isle of Arran cast its enchanting spell upon you.

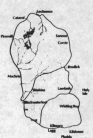

For free full colour brochure
Tel 0770 2140
(24 hours)

Or write to the Isle of Arran Tourist Board,
Tourist Information Centre, Brodick, Isle of Arran.

KINLOCH HOTEL
BLACKWATERFOOT, ISLE OF ARRAN KA27 8ET

49 rooms with private bathroom. Centrally heated throughout. Heated indoor swimming pool, sauna, solarium and squash court. Golf package including car ferry charges and green fees £220 per person for 7 days golf and seven nights dinner, bed & breakfast.

Fully licensed.

Lawrence & Robin Crawford, resident proprietors.

Tel: (0770 86) 286.

CORRIE HOTEL
Corrie, Isle of Arran KA27 8JB

The ideal location for climbing, walking, fishing, pony-trekking, golfing and diving. Family hotel which provides good food and comfort at reasonable prices. Reduced rates and special facilities for families with children. Bar lunches and bar teas. Beer garden on sea front. Open all year round. Resident Proprietors: John and Anne Bruce.

Tel: (077081) 273

FOLLOW THE COUNTRY CODE

SET A GOOD EXAMPLE
AND TRY TO FIT IN WITH THE
LIFE AND WORK OF THE COUNTRYSIDE

RULES OF GOLF
Principal Changes introduced in 1984 Code

Definitions

The Definitions have been placed in un-numbered alphabetical order. Some Definitions are also repeated at the beginning of their relevant Rule.

In the Rules themselves, defined terms which may be important to the application of a Rule are underlined the first time they appear.

Rules

The sequence of the Rules has been rearranged and incorporates certain Decisions made under the rules.

4-1. Form and Make of Clubs

Previously, flat sides were allowed on all grips. In the new Rules, the grips for all clubs, except putters, are required to be generally circular in cross-section. Flat sides will continue to be allowed in putter grips.

5-3 Ball Unfit for Play

Player shall additionally give his opponent, marker or fellow-competitor an opportunity to examine the ball.

6-2b. Handicap – Stroke Play (handicap competition)

Handicap to be recorded on the competitor's score card before it is returned to the Committee.

6-3. Time of Starting

The penalty of disqualification for late starting has been retained. However, a Note has been added to provide that a Committee may, in the conditions of a competition, modify the penalty for being up to five minutes late to loss of the first hole to be played in match play or two strokes in stroke play.

7. Practice

Amended to limit practice between holes to putts or chips on or near the putting green of the hole last played, any practice putting green or the next teeing ground. Such practice strokes must not be played from a hazard.

The prohibition against practice on a competition course before a stroke play round has been expanded to prohibit also the testing of the surface of any putting green on the course before such a round.

8-1. Advice

A Note has been added permitting the Committee in charge of a team competition to allow each team to receive advice from one person such as a team captain or coach. However, this will not be permissible if an individual competition is being held concurrently with the team competition.

10. Order of Play

In all forms of match play, a player may require his opponent to replay a stroke played out of turn. Previously, in the case of three-ball and four-ball matches, a player could not require an opponent to replay a stroke played out of turn from through the green or in a hazard.

There is no penalty in stroke play for playing out of turn from the teeing ground or elsewhere unless competitors have agreed to play out of turn for the purpose of giving one of them an advantage. Previously, there was a penalty for deliberately playing out of turn from the teeing ground.

12-1. Searching for Ball

There is no penalty if a ball lying in casual water, ground under repair or a burrowing animal hole is accidentally moved during search. Previously, the player was exempt from penalty only if his ball was moved in probing for it.

12.2 Identifying Ball

Player shall additionally give his opponent, marker or fellow-competitor an opportunity to observe the lifting and replacement.

14-3. Artificial Devices and Unusual Equipment

Redrafted to include unusual equipment and to apply only during a stipulated round.

18-2. Ball at Rest Moved by Player, etc.

Ball moved without authority and not replaced. In stroke play penalty modified to two strokes.

18-5. Ball at Rest Moved – By Another Ball

In all forms of play, if a player's ball at rest is moved by another ball, the moved ball must be replaced and the other ball played as it lies. There is no penalty except that in stroke play, if both balls lay on the putting green prior to the stroke, the player of the stroke will continue to be subject to a penalty of two strokes. Previously, in singles match play, if a player's ball at rest was moved by his opponent's ball, the player had the option of playing his ball as it lay or replacing it.

20-1. Lifting

Before lifting a ball anywhere on the course which is required to be replaced, its position must be marked.

20-2a. Dropping – By Whom and How

In dropping a ball under a Rule, the player is required to stand erect, hold the ball at shoulder height and arm's length and drop it. There is no restriction on the direction the player faces. If the dropped ball touches the player or his equipment before or after it strikes the ground, the ball must be re-dropped without penalty.

20-3b. Lie of Ball to Be Placed or Replaced Altered

Previously, if the lie of the ball to be placed or replaced was altered, the ball had to be placed in the nearest lie within *two* club-lengths which was most similar to that which it originally occupied. *Two* club-lengths have been reduced to *one* club-length and, in a bunker, the original lie has to be recreated as nearly as possible and the ball placed in that lie.

22. Ball Interfering with or Assisting Play

In all forms of play, an opponent or fellow-competitor is permitted to lift his ball if he considers that it might assist any other player or have any other ball lifted if he considers that it might interfere with his play or assist the play of any other player. Formerly, in singles and foursome match play, if the player considered an opponent's ball might assist him, the player could require his opponent to leave his ball there.

24.2 Immovable Obstructions

If a ball lies in a water hazard, the player is no longer entitled to relief without penalty if his swing or stance is interfered with by an immovable obstruction. On the other hand, if an immovable obstruction on a putting green, such as a sprinkler head, intervenes between a ball on the putting green and the hole, relief is permitted.

24-2b and 25-1b.

Exceptions have been added to the Rules relating to relief from immovable obstructions, casual water, ground under repair and burrowing animal holes to provide there is no relief if (a) it is clearly unreasonable for the player to play a stroke because of interference by any other condition or (b) interference would occur only through use of an unnecessarily abnormal stance, swing or direction of play.

25-1. Casual Water, Ground Under Repair and Certain Damage to Course

If a ball lies in a water hazard, the player is no longer entitled to relief without penalty from a hole made by a burrowing animal, reptile or bird which interferes with his swing or stance.

26-2. Ball Played Within Water Hazard

Incorporates a new provision permitting a player who has played from within a water hazard and failed to cross any margin of the hazard, or is out of bounds, lost or unplayable, a further option under additional penalty to play his next stroke as nearly as possible at the spot from which the last stroke from outside the hazard was played.

29. Threesomes and Foursomes

Amended to allow partners in both match play and stroke play to change the order of teeing off round to round.

30 and 31. Four-Ball Competition

In four-ball match play and stroke play one partner may represent the side for all or any part of a match or round. The absent player/competitor may join his match/partner between the play of any two holes, but not during the play of a hole.

31-4. Four-Ball Stroke Play

The gross scores to count must be individually identifiable on the score card.

Copyright of the Rules of Golf is jointly held by the Royal and Ancient Golf Club of St. Andrews and the United States Golf Association.

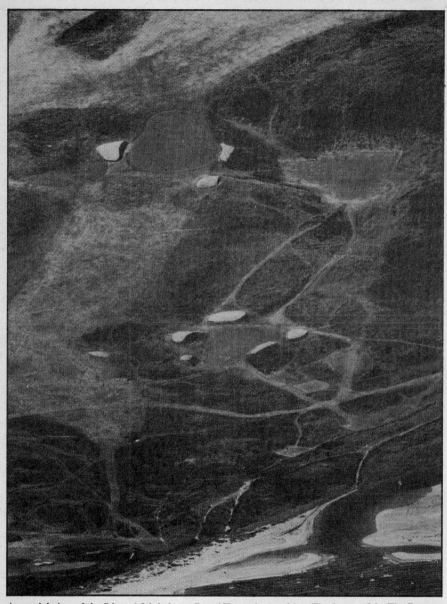

An aerial view of the 7th and 8th holes at Royal Troon in Ayrshire. The famous 8th (The Postage Stamp) on the left is one of the shortest but trickiest holes in championship golf. The tee is in the left foreground, alongside the 7th green.

GOLF COURSES AND CLUBS IN SCOTLAND

MAP OF THE COURSES AND CLUBS

ISLANDS (SHETLAND)

ISLANDS (ORKNEY)

ISLANDS (WESTERN ISLES)

GRAMPIAN

HIGHLAND

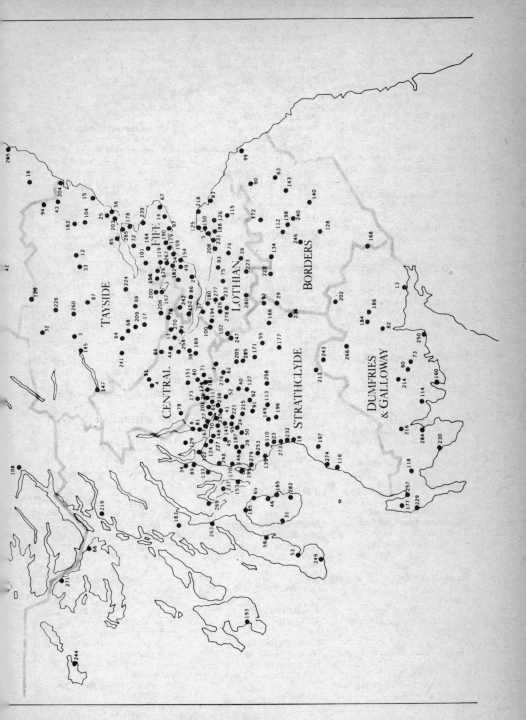

1 Aberdeen
Aberdeenshire

★Kings Links Golf Course
Contact Aberdeen District
Council, Dept. of Leisure &
Recreation, St Nicholas House,
Broad Street, Aberdeen.
Tel: 0224 642121 (Ext. 232).
18 holes, length of course 5838m/
6384 yds.
SSS 70
Charges: £3.60 per round.
A practice area is available.
Professional: Mr Smith

★Bon Accord Golf Club
19 Golf Road, Aberdeen.
Tel: 0224 633464
18 holes, length of course 6368m/
6494 yds.
SSS 71
Charges: £2 per round.
For advance reservations Tel: 0224
633464.
A practice area, caddy cars and
catering facilities are available.
Secretary: Mr A McDonald —
Tel: 0224 34741
Professional: Mr Smith

Westhill Golf Club (1977)
Westhill, Aberdeenshire.
Tel:0224 740159
18 holes, length of course 5866
yds.
SSS 68
Charges: £4.50 round (Mon-Fri),
£5.50 (Sun & Public Holidays),
£8.50 daily (Mon-Fri), £8.50 (Sun
& Public Holidays).
Visitors are welcome all week
except Saturdays.
Secretary: J L Webster
Professional: P McCalla

Balgownie Golf Course
Royal Aberdeen Golf Club
Balgownie, Bridge of Don.
Tel: 0224 702571 (Clubhouse).
(Further details on application)

Murcar Golf Club
Bridge of Don
Aberdeen AB2 8BD
Tel: 0224 704354
18 and 9 holes, length of course
6240 yds.
SSS 70 (Long Tees)
Charges: before 11.30a.m. £7 and
after that £12 round, £12 daily, £35
weekly, £14 Sat/Sun.
For advance reservations Tel: 0224
704370

A practice area, caddy cars and
catering facilities are available.
Visitors are welcome all week
except Saturdays.
Secretary: Lt. Col. R D Strachan
MBE — Tel: 0224 704354
Professional: F J Coutts — Tel:
0224 704370

Deeside Golf Club
Bieldside.
Tel: 0224 867697
(Further details on application)

★Balnagask Golf Club
Nigg Bay Golf Club
St Fittick's Road, Aberdeen.
Tel: 0224 871286
(Further details on application)

2 Aberdour
Fife

Aberdour Golf Club
Seaside Place, Aberdour
Fife KY3 0TX
Tel: 0383 860256
18 holes, length of course
5,001m/ 5,469 yds.
SSS 67
Charges: Mon/Fri £5 round, Sat.
£7 round, Mon/Fri £8 daily, Sat.
£11 daily, £25 weekly.
For advance reservations Tel:
0383 860256
A practice area, caddy cars and
catering facilities are available.
Visitors are welcome all week
except Tues. and Sat.
Secretary: R M Walker — Tel:
0383 860352
Professional: J Bennett — Tel:
0383 860256

3 Aberfeldy
Perthshire

Aberfeldy Golf Course
Taybridge Road, Aberfeldy.
Tel: Aberfeldy 20535
9 holes, length of course 5100m/
5577 yds.
SSS 67
Charges: £5 daily, £16 weekly.

4 Aberfoyle
Stirlingshire

Aberfoyle Golf Club
Braeval, Aberfoyle
Tel: Aberfoyle 493
18 holes, length of course 4760m/
5204 yds.
SSS 66

Charges: £6 daily.
For advance reservations Tel: Mrs.
C Shackleton on Aberfoyle 531.
Visitors are welcome all week.
Secretary: A H McDonald — Tel:
Aberfoyle 441

5 Aberlady
East Lothian

Luffness New Golf Club
The Clubhouse, Aberlady.
Tel: Gullane 843336
18 holes, length of course 6,100
yds.
SSS 69
Charges: £10 round, £14 daily
A practice area, caddy cars and
catering facilities are available.
Visitors are welcome by letter of
introduction with prior notice.
Secretary: R S Murray — Tel:
Gullane 843336

Kilspindie Golf Course
Tel: Aberlady 216
(Further details on application)

6 Aboyne
Aberdeenshire

Aboyne Golf Club
Tel: Aboyne 2328
(Further details on application)

Tarland Golf Club
Tel: Tarland 413
9 holes, length of course (18)
5266m/5758 yds.
SSS 68
(Further details on application)

7 Airdrie
Lanarkshire

Airdrie Golf Club
Glenmavis Road
Airdrie ML6 0PQ
Tel: Airdrie 62195
18 holes, length of course 5471m/
6004 yds.
SSS 67
Charges: £5.35 round, £8.05 daily.
For advance reservations Tel:
Airdrie 62195
Caddy cars and catering facilities
are available.
Secretary: R P Kennedy — Tel:
Airdrie 64864
Professional: T Melville — Tel:
Airdrie 54360

Easter Moffat Golf Club
Mansion House, Plains.
Tel: Caldercruix 842289
18 holes, length of course 5690m/
6222 yds.
SSS 70
Charges: £5 round, £7 daily.
For advance reservations Tel:
Caldercruix 842289.
A practice area, driving range and
caddy cars are available.
Visitors are welcome Monday to
Friday.
Secretary: Mr J Reilly — Tel:
Caldercruix 842289
Professional: Mr D Yates

8 Alexandria
Dunbartonshire

Vale of Leven Golf Club
Northfield Road, Bonhill.
Tel: Alexandria 52351.
(Further details on application)

9 Alloa
Clackmannanshire

Alloa Golf Club
Schaw Park, Sauchie
By Alloa
Tel: 0259 722745
18 holes, length of course 6240
yds.
SSS 70
Charges: £5 round, £7 daily
(1986).
For advance bookings contact the
Secretary.
A practice area, caddy cars and
catering facilities are available.
Visitors are welcome all week
except weekends.
Secretary: A M Frame — Tel:
0259 50100
Professional: Bill Bennett — Tel:
0259 724476

10 Alness
Ross-shire

Alness Golf Club
(Further details on application)

11 Alva
Clackmannanshire

Alva Golf Club
Beanclerc Street, Alva.
9 holes.
Charges: £2 daily (Mon-Fri), £3
(Sat/Sun).
(Further details on application)

12 Alyth
Perthshire

The Alyth Golf Club
Pitcrocknie, Alyth.
Tel: Alyth 2268.
18 holes, length of course 5689m/
6226 yds.
SSS 70 (Boxes 68)
Charges: Mon-Fri £6 round, Sat/
Sun £9 round, Mon-Fri £9 daily,
Sat/Sun £12 daily, £25 weekly.
For advance reservations Tel:
Alyth 2268.
A practice area, caddy cars and
catering facilities are available.
Visitors are welcome all week.
Secretary: Mr G B Crichton —
Tel: Alyth 2268
Professional: Mr B Young — Tel:
Alyth 2268

13 Annan
Dumfriesshire

Powfoot Golf Club
Powfoot, Annan.
Tel: Cummertrees 227
18 holes, length of course 5465m/
5977 yds.
SSS 69
Charges: Mon-Fri £8 round or Sat/
Sun £10 daily, £32 weekly.
For advance reservations Tel:
Annan 2866/7.
A practice area, caddy cars and
catering facilities are available.
Visitors are welcome all week
except Sundays.
Secretary: R G Anderson — Tel:
Annan 2866/7
Professional: Lee Johnson — Tel:
Cummertrees 327

14 Anstruther
Fife

Anstruther Golf Club
Marsfield, Shore Road,
Anstruther.
9 holes.
SSS 63
Charges: Sat/Sun £4 round, Mon-
Fri £2.50 daily (1986).
For advance reservations Tel: 0333
310 224.
Catering facilities are available.
Visitors are welcome all week.
Secretary: T Reid — Tel: 0333 310
224

15 Arbroath
Angus

★**Arbroath Golf Course (Public)**
(Further details on application)

Letham Grange Golf Club
Colliston, By Arbroath DD11 4RL
(Further details on application)

16 Auchenblae
Kincardineshire

Auchenblae Golf Course
Auchenblae Golf Club
Auchenblae.
Tel: Auchenblae 407
9 holes, length of course 2174 yds.
SSS 30
Charges: £2.50 round, except
Sunday which is £3 round, £2.50
daily, except Sunday which is £3
daily.
Visitors are welcome all week
except Wednesday and Friday
nights when the course can get
very crowded as members hold
competitions these nights.
Secretary: Mr. A Robertson —
Tel: Auchenblae 407.

17 Auchterarder
Perthshire

Gleneagles Hotel Golf Courses
Gleneagles Hotel
Auchterarder PH3 1NF
Tel: 076 46 3543
There are four 18 hole golf
courses:
King's Course: length of course
5906m/6452 yds.
SSS 71, Par 70
Queen's Course: length of course
5455m/5964 yds.
SSS 69, Par 68
Glendevon Course: length of
course 5230m/5719 yds.
SSS 68, Par 67
Prince's Course: length of course
4238m/4664 yds.
SSS 64, Par 63
Charges on Application.
For advance reservations Tel: 076
46 3543.
A practice area, caddies, caddy
cars and catering facilities are
available.
Visitors are welcome throughout
the week and at weekends.
However, tees are reserved on the
Kings and Queens Courses before
10.30am and between 1.30pm and
2.30pm each day for hotel
residents and members only.

Sports Manager: Mr. I Bulleid —
Tel: 076 46 3543
Professional: Mr. I Marchbank —
Tel: 076 46 3543

Auchterarder Golf Club
Orchil Road, Auchterarder.
Tel: Auchterarder 2804
18 holes, length of course 5737
yds.
SSS 68
Charges: £6 daily and £7 weekly.
For advance reservations Tel:
Auchterarder 2804.
A practice area, caddy cars and
catering facilities are available.
Visitors are welcome all week.
Secretary: Mr. J I Stewart — Tel:
Auchterarder 3840

18 Ayr
Ayrshire

★Belleisle Golf Club
Doonfoot Road, Ayr.
Tel: 0292 41258
18 holes, length of course 5978m/
6540 yds.
SSS 71
Charges: £4.30 round, £5.30
round, (Sat/Sun), £5.70 daily,
£8.60 daily (Sat/Sun), £25.90
weekly. (This is a local authority
owned course - charges are
reviewed annually).
For advance reservations Tel: 0292
41258.
A practice area, caddy cars and
catering facilities are available.
Visitors are welcome all week.
Hon. Secretary: A F Wilson
Professional: Mr. J S Easy — Tel:
0292 41314

★Dalmilling Golf Course
Westwood Avenue
Ayr
Tel: 0292 263893
18 holes, length of course 5401
yds.
SSS 66
Charges: £3.50 round, £4.40 daily,
£25.90 weekly.
For advance reservations Tel: 0292
263893.
Caddy cars and catering facilities
are available.
Visitors are welcome all week.
Secretary: Mr. C King – Tel: 0292
268180
Professional: D Gemmell – Tel:
0292 263893

19 Ballater
Aberdeenshire

Ballater Golf Club
Victoria Road, Ballater.
Tel: 0338 55567
18 holes, length of course 5704
yds.
SSS 67
Charges: Mon - Fri £6 daily, Sat/
Sun £7.50 daily, £20.50 weekly.
For advance reservations Tel: 0338
55567/55658.
A practice area, caddy cars and
catering facilities are available.
Visitors are welcome Monday to
Friday.
Secretary: A Ingram – Tel: 0338
55567
Professional: F Mann – Tel: 0338
55658

20 Balmore
Stirlingshire

Balmore Golf Club
Balmore, Torrance.
Tel: Balmore 21240
18 holes, length of course 5735
metres.
SSS 67
Charges: £8 round, £10 daily, £50
weekly.
For advance reservations Tel: 041
332 0392.
A practice area, caddy cars and
catering facilities are available.
Visitors are welcome Monday -
Friday.
Secretary: G P Woolard – Tel: 041
332 0392

21 Banchory
Kincardineshire

Banchory Golf Club
Kinneskie Road, Banchory.
Tel: Banchory 2365
18 holes, length of course 4833m/
5284 yds.
Charges: Mon - Fri (after 3p.m.)
£6 round, Mon - Fri £8 daily, Sat/
Sun £10 daily, £30 weekly.
For advance reservations Tel:
Banchory 2447.
A practice area, caddy cars and
catering facilities are available.
Visitors are welcome all week
except Thursdays and Saturdays.
Secretary: Mr S A J Adamson –
Tel: Banchory 2365
Professional Mr D W Smart – Tel:
Banchory 2447

22 Banff
Bannfshire

Duff House Royal Golf Club
The Barnyards, Banff.
Tel: 02612 2062.
18 holes, length of course 6161
yds.
SSS 69
Charges: £5 (weekday) round, £6
(weekend) round, £6.50 (weekday)
daily, £7.50 (weekend) daily.
For advance reservations Tel:
02612 2062.
A practice area, caddy cars and
catering facilities are available.
Visitors are welcome all week (but
within restricted times, as shown
on Tee Booking sheets).
Secretary: M Pierog – Tel: 02614
3835
Professional: R S Strachan – Tel:
02612 2075

23 Barassie
Troon, Ayrshire

Kilmarnock (Barassie) Golf Club
29 Hillhouse Road, Barassie,
Troon CA10 6SY.
Tel: Troon 313920
18 holes, length of course 5896m/
6450 yds.
SSS 71
Charges: £15 round, £15 daily
(1986)
For advance reservations Tel:
Troon 313920.
A practice area, caddies, caddy
cars and catering facilities are
available.
Visitors are welcome
Mon/Tues/Thur/Fri.
Secretary: M Davis – Tel: Troon
313920
Professional W R Lockie – Tel:
Troon 311322

24 Barrhead
Renfrewshire

Fereneze Golf Club
Fereneze Avenue, Barrhead.
Tel: 041 881 1519.
(This is a Strictly Private Club)

25 Barry
Angus

Panmure Golf Club
Burnside Road, Carnoustie.
Tel: Carnoustie 53120

18 holes, length of course 5761m/
6302 yds.
SSS 70
Charges on application.
For advance reservations Tel:
Carnoustie 53705/52374.
A practice area, caddy cars and
catering facilities are available
(Except Mondays).
Visitors are welcome all week
except Saturdays.
Secretary: Captain J C Ray — Tel:
Carnoustie 53705
Professional: T Shiel — Tel:
Carnoustie 52374

26 Bathgate
West Lothian

Bathgate Golf Course
Edinburgh Road, Bathgate.
Tel: Bathgate 52232
18 holes, length of course 6325
yds.
SSS 70
£5 daily (Mon-Fri), £7 (Sat/Sun).
For advance reservations Tel:
Bathgate 630505.
A practice area, caddy cars and
catering facilities are available.
Secretary: Mr J Connor — Tel:
Bathgate 630505
Professional: D R W Strachan —
Tel: Bathgate 630553

27 Bearsden
Dunbartonshire

Windyhill Golf Club
Windyhill, Bearsden G61 4QQ.
Tel: 041 942 2349
18 holes, length of course 6254
yds.
SSS 70
Charges: £7 daily.
For advance reservations contact
the Secretary by letter.
A practice area, caddy cars and
catering facilities are available.
Visitors are welcome all week
except Sat/Sun, by prior
arrangement.
Secretary: Mr P O Bell – Tel: 041
942 2349
Professional: R Collinson – Tel:
041 942 7157

Douglas Park Golf Course
Hillfoot, Bearsden.
Tel: 041 942 2220
(Further details on application)

Bearsden Golf Club
Thorn Road, Bearsden, Glasgow.
Tel: 041 942 2351
9 holes, length of course 5465m/
5977 yds.
SSS 69
Catering facilities are available.
Visitors introduced by members
are welcome all week.
Secretary: J D McArthur – Tel:
041 942 1642

28 Beith
Ayrshire

Beith Golf Club
Threepwood Road, Bigholm,
Beith.
Tel: Beith 3166
(Further details on application)

29 Biggar
Lanarkshire

Biggar Golf Club
The Park, Broughton Road,
Biggar.
Tel: 0899 20618
18 holes, length of course 4800m/
5258 yds.
SSS 66
Charges: Adults from Oct - March
£3 any day, Summer £3.50
weekdays and £5.50 Sat/Sun.
For advance reservations Tel: 0899
20319.
Caddy cars and catering facilities
are available. (no catering
Mondays).
Visitors are welcome all week.
Secretary: W S Turnbull – Tel:
0899 20566

★**Biggar Municipal Golf Course**
Public Park, Broughton Road,
Biggar.
Tel: Biggar 20319.
(Further details on application)

Leadhills Golf Course
Leadhills, Lanarkshire.
Tel: Leadhills 222.
(Further details on application)

30 Bishopton
Renfrewshire

Erskine Golf Club
(Further details on application)

31 Blackwaterfoot
Isle of Arran

Shiskine Golf and Tennis Club
Tel: Shiskine 226
(Further details on application)

32 Blair Atholl
Perthshire

Blair Atholl Golf Course
Tel: Blair Atholl 407
(Further details on application)

33 Blairgowrie
Perthshire

Dalmunzie Golf Course
Spittal of Glenshee, Blairgowrie.
Tel: 025 085 226
9 holes, length of course 1861m/
2035 yds.
SSS 31 (62 for 18 – to be
confirmed by SGU).
Charges: £2 for 9 holes round, £3
daily, £16 weekly.
For advance reservations Tel: 025
085 226.
A practice area and catering
facilities are available.
Visitors are welcome all week.
Secretary: Mr S N Winton – Tel:
025 085 226

34 Blairmore
By Dunoon, Argyll

Blairmore & Strone Golf Course
Blairmore, By Dunoon.
Tel: Kilmun 676
9 holes, length of course 1933m/
2112 yds.
SSS 62
Charges: £2 round, £2 daily, £8
weekly.
Visitors are welcome all week
except Saturday afternoons.
Secretary: A B Horton – Tel:
Kilmun 217

35 Boat of Garten
Inverness-shire

Boat of Garten Golf Club
Tel: 047 983 282
18 holes, length of course 5690
yds.
SSS 68
Charges: Mon - Fri £5 daily, Sat/
Sun £6 daily, £25 weekly.
For advance reservations Tel: 047
983 282 (at weekends – starting
sheet in use).

Caddies, caddy cars and catering facilities are available.
Visitors are welcome all week.
Secretary: J R Ingram – Tel: 047 983 282/351/684

36 Bonar Bridge
Sutherland

Bonar Bridge – Ardgay Golf Club
Bonar Bridge.
9 holes, length of course 4626 yds.
SSS Men 63, Ladies 66.
Charges: £2.50 daily, £12 weekly
For advance reservations Tel: 086 32 577 or 054 982 248 (Groups only)
Visitors are welcome all week.
Secretaries: A Turner – Tel: 054 982 248
Mrs J Gordon – Tel: 086 32 577

37 Bo'ness
West Lothian

West Lothian Golf Club
Airngath Hill, Linlithgow.
Tel: Bo'ness 826030.
18 holes, length of course 6578 yds.
SSS 72
Charges: £4 round, £6 daily, £30 weekly.
For advance reservations Tel: Bo'ness 826030.
A practice area and catering facilities are available.
Visitors are welcome all week.
(Tel. in advance for week-ends).
Secretary: Mr J W Blair – Tel: Bo'ness 823711

38 Bonnybridge
Stirlingshire

Bonnybridge Golf Club
(Further details on application)

39 Bonnyrigg
Midlothian

Broomieknowe Golf Club
36 Golf Course Road, Bonnyrigg EH19 2HZ.
Tel: 031 663 9317.
18 holes, length of course 5526m/ 6046 yds.
SSS 69
Charges: £6 round, £7 daily.
For advance reservations Tel: 031 663 9317.

A practice area, caddy cars and catering facilities are available.
Visitors are welcome Monday – Friday.
Secretary: Mr I Lawson – Tel:031 663 9317
Professional: Mr M Patchett – Tel: 031 660 2035

40 Bothwell
Lanarkshire

Bothwell Castle Golf Club
Blantyre Road, Bothwell, Glasgow G71.
Tel: Bothwell 85 3177.
18 holes, length of course 5881m/ 6432 yds.
SSS 71
Charges: £5 round, £7 daily.
For advance reservations Tel: Bothwell 85 2052.
A practice area, caddy cars and catering facilities are available.
Visitors are welcome Monday – Friday.
Secretary: A D C Watson – Tel: Bothwell 85 2395
Professional Mr W Walker – Tel: Bothwell 85 2052

41 Braehead
By Paisley, Renfrewshire.

The Paisley Golf Course
Braehead, By Paisley.
Tel: 041 884 3903
18 holes, length of course 5857m/ 6424 yds.
SSS 71
Charges: £6 round, £8 daily (Subject to revision).
For advance reservations Tel: 041 884 3903.
A practice area and catering facilities are available.
Visitors are welcome Monday to Friday.
Secretary: W J Cunningham — Tel: 041 884 3903

42 Braemar
Aberdeenshire

Braemar Golf Course
Cluniebank Road, Braemar.
Tel: 033 83 618.
18 holes, length of course 5011 yds.
SSS 64
Charges: £4.50 round, £7 daily, £20 weekly.

For advance reservations Tel: 033 83 618.
A practice area and catering facilities are available.
Visitors are welcome all week (booking essential for weekends).
Secretary: Mr G A McIntosh – Tel: 0224 868535

43 Brechin
Angus

Brechin Golf and Squash Club
Trinity, By Brechin DDH 7PD.
Tel: 035 62 2383.
18 holes, length of course 5267 yds.
SSS 66
Charges: £4 (Mon-Fri) round, £5 (Sat/Sun) round, £6 (Mon-Fri) daily, £8 (Sat/Sun) daily, £20 weekly (Monday – Friday only).
For advance reservations Tel: Brechin 9035 62 2383.
A practice area, caddy cars and catering facilities are available.
Visitors are welcome all week.
Secretary: D A Milligan – Tel: Brechin 4969
Professional: Pro's Shop – Tel: Brechin 5270

44 Bridge of Allan
Stirlingshire

Bridge of Allan Golf Club
Sunnylaw, Bridge of Allan, Stirling.
Tel: Bridge of Allan 832332.
9 holes, length of course 4508m/ 4932 yds.
SSS 65
Charges: £3 round.
A practice area is available.
Visitors are welcome all week except Saturday.
Secretary: G Cruickshank – Tel: Bridge of Allan 833087

45 Bridge of Weir
Renfrewshire

Ranfurly Castle Golf Club Ltd
Golf Road, Bridge of Weir.
Tel: Bridge of Weir 612609.
18 holes, length of course 6284 yds.
SSS 70
Charges: On Application.
A practice area, caddy cars and catering facilities are available.
Visitors are welcome Monday to

Friday (to be previously arranged with Secretary).
Secretary: Mrs T J Gemmell – Tel: Bridge of Weir 612609
Professional Mr K Stables – Tel: Bridge of Weir 614795

46 Brodick
Isle of Arran

Machrie Bay Golf Club
Machrie Bay, Brodick.
Tel: Machrie 258
9 holes, length of course 1904m/2082 yds.
SSS 31
Charges: £1 round, £1 daily.
For advance reservations Tel: Machrie 258.
Catering facilities are available from June to September.
Secretary: Mr J M Buchanan — Machrie 258.

Brodick Golf Club
Brodick, Isle of Arran.
Tel: 0770 2349.
18 holes, length of course 4402 yds.
SSS 62
Charges: £3.50 round (restricted hours), £5 daily, £22 weekly.
For advance reservations Tel: 0770 2513.
A practice area, caddy cars and catering facilities are available.
Visitors are welcome all week.
Secretary: Mr G I Jameson – Tel: 0770 2225
Professional: Mr D J Pirie – Tel: 0770 2513

47 Brora
Sutherland

Brora Golf Club
Golf Road, Brora KW9 6QS.
Tel: Brora 21417.
18 holes, length of course 6110 yds.
SSS 69
Charges: £5 round, £5 daily, £20 weekly, £30 fortnightly, £35 three weekly, £40 monthly.
For advance reservations Tel: Brora 21417/21475.
A practice area, caddy cars and catering facilities (May - Aug) are available.
Visitors are welcome all week (except Tournament days).
Secretary: R D Smith – Tel: Brora 21475

48 Buckie
Banffshire

Strathlene Golf Club
Tel: Buckie 31798
SSS 69
(Further details on application)

Buckpool Golf Club
Barhill Road, Buckie.
Tel: 0542 32236.
18 holes, length of course 6257 yds.
SSS 70
Charges: £4 (day ticket, Mon-Fri) round, £6 (day ticket, Sat/Sun) daily, £20 weekly (Concessionary rates for under 18 years old).
For advance reservations Tel: 0542 32236.
Catering facilities are available.
Visitors are welcome all week (prior arrangement).
Secretary: Mr F MacLeod OBE – Tel: 0542 35368.

49 Burntisland
Fife

Burntisland Golf House Club
Dodhead, Burntisland.
Tel: 0592 874093.
18 holes, length of course 5369m/5871 yds.
SSS 68
Charges: £5 (weekday) round, £8 (Sat/Sun) round, £7 (weekday) daily, £11 (Sat/Sun) daily (1986), weekly by arrangement.
For advance reservations Tel: 0592 873247/874093.
A practice area, caddy cars and catering facilities are available.
Visitors are welcome all week.
Secretary: M W Mann – Tel: 0592 874093
Professional Mr J C Macdonald – Tel: 0592 873247

50 Caldwell
Renfrewshire

Caldwell Golf Club Ltd
(Further details on application)

51 Callander
Perthshire

Callander Golf Club
Aveland Road, Callander FK17 8EN.
Tel: 0877 30090.
18 holes, length of course 4060/4677m/4445/5125 yds.
SSS 63/66
For advance reservations Tel: 0877 30975/30090.
A practice area, caddy cars and catering facilities are available.
Visitors are welcome all week.
Secretary: H G Slater – Tel: 0877 30931 (Home).
Professional Mr J McCallum – Tel: 0877 30975

52 Cambuslang
Glasgow

Cambuslang Golf Club
(Further details on application)

53 Campbeltown
Argyllshire

The Machrihanish Golf Club
Machrihanish, By Campbeltown.
Tel: Machrihanish 213.
18 and 9 holes, length of course 6228 yds.
SSS 70
Charges: £7.50 (18), £4 (9) round, £8.50 (18), £4 (9) daily, £37.50 (18), £12 (9) weekly, £9.50 (Sat/Sun).
For advance reservations Tel: Machrihanish 213.
A practice area, caddy cars and catering facilities are available.
Visitors are welcome all week.
Secretary: Machrihanish 213
Professional: Mr A Thomson – Tel: Machrihanish 217

54 Cardenden
Fife

Auchterderran Golf Club
Woodend Road, Cardenden.
Tel: Cardenden 721579.
9 holes, length of course 5250 yds.
SSS 66
Charges: £2.10 (Mon-Fri) round, £3.20 (Sat/Sun) daily.
For advance reservations Tel: Cardenden 721579.
A practice area, caddy cars and catering facilities are available.
Visitors are welcome all week.
Secretary: Mr S M Miller – Tel: Cardenden 721579
Professional: Mr J Smith – Tel: Cardenden 721579

55 Carluke
Lanarkshire

Carluke Golf Club
Mauldslie Road, Hallcraig,
Carluke ML8 5HG.
Tel: 0555 71 070.
18 holes, length of course 5308m/
5805 yds.
SSS 68
Charges: £6 round, £9 daily.
For advance reservations Tel: (Pro
Shop) 0555 51 053.
A practice area and catering
facilities are available.
Visitors are welcome all week
except Sat/Sun.
Secretary: J Kyle – Tel: 0555 70
366
Professional: A Brooks – Tel: 0555
51 053

56 Carnoustie
Angus

Carnoustie Golf Club
Links Parade.
Tel: 0241 52486
Secretary: D W Curtis.

★Dalhousie Golf Club
Links Parade.
Tel: 0241 53208
(Further details on application)

★Mercantile Golf Club
Links Parade.
Tel: 0241 52525
Secretary: M W Sullivan – Tel:
0241 53159

★New Taymouth Golf Club
Taymouth Street.
Tel: 0241 52425
(Further details on application)

Caledonia Golf Club
Links Parade.
Tel: 0241 52112
(Further details on application)

★Burnside Golf Course
Links Parade.
Tel: Carnoustie 53789
(Further details on application)

★Carnoustie Medal Golf Course
The Links, Carnoustie.
Tel: Carnoustie 53249
18 holes, length of course 6226m/
6809 yds.

Charges: £12 (Mon-Fri), £14 (Sat/
Sun), £45 weekly.
For advance reservations Tel:
Carnoustie 53789 (Secretary).
Caddies and caddy cars are
available.

Buddon Links
Tel: 0241 53249
(Further details on application)

57 Carnwath
Lanarkshire

Carnwath Golf Course
1 Main Street, Carnwath,.
Tel: Carnwath 251
(Further details on application)

58 Carradale
Argyll

Carradale Golf Course
Carradale, Kintyre.
Tel: 05833 624.
9 holes, length of course 2387 yds.
SSS 63
Charges: £2 round, £3 daily, £12
weekly.
For advance reservations Tel: 0583
3624.
Visitors are welcome all week.
Secretary: J Taylor

59 Carrbridge
Inverness-shire

★Carrbridge Golf Club
Carrbridge.
Tel: Carrbridge 202
(Further details on application)

60 Castle Douglas
Kirkcudbrightshire

Castle Douglas Golf Course
Abercromby Road, Castle
Douglas.
Tel: Castle Douglas 2801
(Further details on application)

61 Clydebank
Dunbartonshire

Clydebank & District Golf Club
(Further details on application)

62 Coatbridge
Lanarkshire

Coatbridge Golf Club
Townhead Road, Coatbridge.
Tel: Coatbridge 28975
(Further details on application)

Drumpellier Golf Club
Langloan, Coatbridge,
Lanarkshire.
Tel: 0236 28723.
18 holes, length of course 6227
yds.
SSS 70
Charges: £7 round, £9 daily.
For advance reservations Tel: 0236
23065/28538.
A practice area, caddy cars and
catering facilities are available.
Visitors are welcome Mondays,
Tuesdays and Fridays.
Secretary: Mr Wm Brownlie —
Tel: 0236 23065
Professional: Mr I Collins — Tel:
0236 32971

63 Coldstream
Berwickshire

Hirsel Golf Club
Kelso Road, Coldstream.
Tel: 0890 2678
9 holes.
SSS 68 (72 Ladies)
Charges: £3.50 round, £4.50
weekends.
For advance reservations Tel: 0890
2251.
A practice area and catering
facilities (summer only) are
available.
Visitors are welcome all week.
Secretary: I Sproule – Tel: 0890
2251

64 Comrie
Perthshire

Comrie Golf Club
c/o Secretary, 10 Polinard,
Comrie.
Tel: Comrie 70544.
9 holes, length of course 5962 yds.
SSS 69
Charges: £3 daily (£4 - weekends
and holidays), £12 weekly.
For advance reservations Tel:
Comrie 70544.
A practice area, caddy cars and
catering facilities are available.
Visitors are welcome all week

except Monday evenings from
4.30p.m.
Secretary: Mr D G McGlashan
Professional: Mr H Donaldson —
Tel: Comrie 70544

65 Corrie
Isle of Arran

Corrie Golf Club
Corrie, Isle of Arran.
(Further details on application)

66 Craignure
Isle of Mull

Craignure Gold Club
Scallastle, Craignure, Isle of Mull
Hotel.
Tel: 068 02 351.
9 holes, length of course 2454 yds.
SSS 66
Charges: £2.50 daily, £10 weekly.
Advance bookings are not
required.
Visitors are welcome all week.
Secretary: Sheila Campbell — Tel:
068 02 370.

67 Crail
Fife

Crail Golfing Society
Balcomie Club House
Fifeness, Crail, Fife KY10 3XN.
Tel: 0333 50278.
18 holes, length of course 5228m/
5720 yds.
SSS 68
Charges: On Application.
For advance reservations Tel: 0333
50686.
A practice area, caddy cars and
catering facilities are available.
Visitors are welcome all week.
Secretary: G Thomson — Tel:
0333 50686

68 Crieff
Perthshire

Crieff Golf Club Ltd
Perth Road, Crieff PH7 3LR.
Tel: 0764 2397.
Ferntower Course:
18 holes, length of course 6419
yds.
SSS 71
Charges: On Application.
Dornock Course:
9 holes, length of course 2386 yds.
SSS 63

Charges: On Application.
For advance reservations Tel: 0764
2909.
A practice area, caddy cars and
catering facilities are available.
Visitors are welcome all week (it is
advisable to book well in
advance).
Secretary: A H Smith — Tel: 0764
2546 (Home)
Professional: Mr J Stark — Tel:
0764 2909

69 Cruden Bay
Aberdeenshire

Cruden Bay Golf Club
Aulton Road, Cruden Bay.
Tel: Cruden Bay 2285
(Further details on application)

70 Cullen
Banffshire

Cullen Golf Club
The Links, Cullen, Buckie.
Tel: Cullen 40685.
18 holes, length of course 4610
yds.
SSS 62
Charges: £3.50 daily
(Mon,Tues,Wed & Thurs) £4 Sat/
Sun, £18 weekly.
Catering facilities are available.
Secretary: Mr J Douglas — Tel:
Cullen 40531.

71 Cumbernauld
Dunbartonshire

★Palacerigg Golf Course
(Further details on application)

72 Cupar
Fife

Cupar Golf Course
Cupar.
(Further details on application)

73 Dalbeattie
Kirkcudbrightshire

Colvend Golf Club
Sandyhills, Colvend, By
Dalbeattie.
Tel: Rockcliffe (Kirkcudbright)
398.
9 holes, length of course 2322 yds.
SSS 63

Charges: £5 daily.
For advance reservations Tel: The
Secretary on Kippford 685.
Catering facilities are available.
Visitors are welcome all week.
Secretary: Mr D McNeil — Tel:
Kippford 685

Dalbeattie Golf Club
(Further details on application

74 Dalkeith
Midlothian

Newbattle Golf Club Ltd
Abbey Road, Dalkeith,
Midlothian.
Tel: 031 663 2123.
18 holes, length of course 5498m/
6012 yds.
SSS 69
Charges: £5.50 round, £7.50 daily
(1986).
For advance reservations Tel: 031
660 1631.
A practice area, caddy cars and
catering facilities are available.
Visitors are welcome all week
except Weekends and Public
holidays.
Secretary: Mr D M Henderson —
Tel: 031 445 3546
Professional Mr J Henderson —
Tel: 031 660 1631

75 Dalmahoy
Kirknewton, Midlothian.

Dalmahoy Golf Course
Dalmahoy Golf Country Club
Tel: 031 333 2055/1436
18 x 2 holes, length of courses East
6097m/6664 yds, West 4767m/5212
yds.
SSS East 72, West 66.
Charges on application.
A practice area, caddy cars,
catering facilities and
accommodation are available.
Visitors are welcome all week.
Secretary: Mrs I Auld

76 Dollar
Clackmannanshire

Dollar Golf Course
Brewlands House, Dollar FK14
7EA.
Tel: 025 94 2400.
18 holes, length of course 5144
yds.
SSS 66

Charges: £3.50 (Mon-Fri) round, £5.50 (Sat/Sun) round, £4.50 (Mon-Fri) daily, £5.50 (Sat/Sun) daily.
For advance reservations Tel: 025 94 2400.
Catering facilities are available.
Visitors are welcome all week.
Secretary: Mr A Porteous — Tel: 025 94 2400

77 Dornoch
Sutherland

Royal Dornoch Golf Club
Golf Road, Dornoch.
Tel: 0862 810 219
(Further details on application)

78 Drymen
Stirlingshire

Buchanan Castle Golf Club
Drymen.
Tel: 0360 60369/07/30.
18 holes, length of course 6032 yds.
SSS 69
Charges: £10 round, £15 daily.
For advance reservations Tel: 0360 60307.
Visitors are welcome by arrangement.
Secretary: Mr J I Hay — Tel: 0360 60307
Professional: Mr C Dernie — Tel: 0360 60330

Strathendrick Golf Club
9 holes, length of course 2636m/ 2433 yds.
SSS 65
For advance reservations Tel: 041 942 3353
Visitors are welcome with a member only.

79 Dufftown
Banffshire

Dufftown Golf Club
(Further details on application)

80 Dullatur
Nr. Cumbernauld, Dunbartonshire.

Dullatur Golf Club
Tel: Cumbernauld 23230
18 holes, length of course 5664m/ 6195 yds.
SSS 70

Charges: £5 round after 1p.m., £7.50 daily.
Caddy cars and catering facilities are available.
Visitors are welcome Monday to Friday.
Secretary: W Laing
Professional: D Sinclair

81 Dumbarton
Dunbartonshire

Dumbarton Golf Course
Broadmeadow, Dumbarton.
Tel: Dumbarton 32830
18 holes, length of course 5469m/ 5981 yds.
SSS 69
Charges: £8 round, £8 daily.
For advance reservations Tel: Dumbarton 32830.
Catering facilities available by prior arrangement.
Visitors are welcome Monday to Friday.
Secretary: Mr J Campbell – Tel: Dumbarton 32830

Cardross Golf Club
Main Road, Cardross, Dumbarton G82 5LB.
Tel: Cardross 841213.
18 holes, length of course 6466 yds.
SSS 71
Charges: £8.50 round, £12.50 daily.
For advance reservations Tel Cardross 841350.
A practice area, caddy cars and catering facilities are available.
Visitors are welcome Monday to Friday.
Secretary: R Evans — Tel: Cardross 841754
Professional: Mr N Cameron — Tel: Cardross 841350

82 Dumfries
Dumfriesshire

Dumfries and County Golf Club
Edinburgh Road, Dumfries DG1 1JX.
Tel: 0387 53585.
18 holes, length of course 5928 yds.
SSS 68
Charges: £7 (Sun £8.50) round, £7 (Sun £8.50) daily, £25 weekly.
A practice area, caddy cars and catering facilities are available.

Visitors are welcome all week (except Saturdays).
Secretary: J K Wells — Tel: 0387 53585
Professional: Mr G Gray — Tel: 0387 68918

83 Dunbar
East Lothian

Dunbar Golf Club
East Links, Dunbar EH42 1LP.
Tel: 0368 62317.
18 holes, length of course 5874m/ 6426 yds.
SSS 71
Charges: £8.50 (£11 weekends) daily, £35 weekly (1986).
For advance reservations Tel: 0368 62317.
A practice area, caddies (if reserved) and catering facilities are available.
Visitors are welcome all week after 9.30a.m.
Secretary: Mr A J R Poole — Tel: 0368 62317
Professional: Mr D Small — Tel: 0368 62086

★Winterfield Golf Club
North Road, Dunbar.
Tel: 0368 62280
18 holes.
SSS 65
Charges: £3.30 round (Mon-Fri), £4 (Sat/Sun), £4.50 daily, £11 weekly (5 days).
For advance reservations Tel: 0368 63562.
Caddy cars and catering facilities are available.
Secretary: Mr M O'Donnell – Tel: 0368 62564
Professional: Mr A Minto

84 Dunblane
Perthshire

Dunblane New Golf Club
Perth Road, Dunblane.
Tel: Dunblane 822 343
18 holes, length of course 5371m/ 5874 yds.
SSS 68
Charges: £4.50 round (Mon-Fri), £8.50 (Sat/Sun), £8 daily.
(Charges subject to revision)
For advance reservations Tel: Dunblane 823217.
A practice area, caddy cars and catering facilities (by advance order) are available.

Visitors are welcome Monday to
Friday.
Secretary: Mr J Allan – Tel:
Dunblane 823217
Professional: R M Jamieson

85 Dundee
Angus

★Camperdown Golf Course
Camperdown Park, Dundee.
Tel: 0382 645457/23141 (Ext. 413).
(Further details on application)

Downfield Golf Course
Turnberry Avenue, Dundee.
Tel: 0382 825595
18 holes, length of course 6306m/
6899 yds.
SSS 73
Charges on appliction.
A practice area, a driving range,
caddy cars and catering facilities
are available.
Visitors are welcome Monday to
Friday.

86 Dunfermline
Fife

Dunfermline Golf Club
Pitfirrane House, Crossford,
Dunfermline.
Tel: Dunfermline 723534
(Further details on application)

Canmore Golf Club
Venturefair, Dunfermline.
Tel: Dunfermline 724969
(Further details from the Secretary
on Dunfermline 726098)

**Pitreavie (Dunfermline) Golf
Club**
Queensferry Road, Dunfermline
KY11 5PR.
Tel: 0383 722591.
18 holes, length of course 5565m/
6086 yds.
SSS 69
Charges: £4.50 (weekdays) round,
£6.50 (weekdays) daily, £10
(weekend) daily.
For advance reservations —
Casual visitors Tel: 0383 723151,
Parties, Societies etc Tel: 0383
722591.
A practice area, caddy cars and
catering facilities are available.
Visitors are welcome all week.
Secretary: W P Syme — Tel: 0383
722591
Professional: Mr A Hope — Tel:
0383 723151

87 Dunkeld
Perthshire

Dunkeld & Birnam Golf CLub
Fungarth, Dunkeld.
Tel: Dunkeld 524
9 holes, length of course 4813m/
5264 yds.
SSS 66
Charges: £3 daily (Mon-Fri), £4.50
(Sat), £5 (Sun).
For advance reservations Tel:
Dunkeld 673.
Caddy cars and catering facilities
are available.
Secretary: Mrs F M Nunn – Tel:
Dunkeld 673

88 Dunning
Perthshire

Dunning Golf Club
Rollo Recreation Ground,
Dunning.
(Further details on application)

89 Dunoon
Argyll

Cowal Golf Club
Ardenslate Road, Dunoon.
Tel: Dunoon 2216
18 holes, length of course 5716m/
6251 yds.
SSS 70
Charges: £6.95 daily.
For advance reservations Tel:
Dunoon 5673.
Caddy cars and catering facilities
(except Mondays) are available.
Secretary: Mr M McMartin – Tel:
Dunoon 5673
Professional: R D Weir

90 Duns
Berwickshire

Duns Golf Club
Hardens Road, Duns.
9 holes, length of course 5826 yds.
SSS 68
Charges: £4 (£5 weekends) round
or daily (half rate Nov — March).
For advance reservations Tel:
Duns 83377.
A practice area is available.
Light refreshments are available
by arrangement.
Visitors are welcome all week
except Tuesday Evenings when
club competitions are held.
Secretary: Mr F Whyte — Tel:
Duns 83377

91 Eaglesham
Renfrewshire

Bonnyton Golf Club
Tel: Eaglesham 2781
(Further details on application)

92 East Kilbride
Lanarkshire

East Kilbride Golf Club
East Kilbride, Glasgow G74 4PF.
Tel: 03552 20913.
18 holes, length of course 6419
yds.
SSS 71
Charges: £5 round, £8 daily.
For advance reservations Tel:
03552 20913.
A practice area, caddy cars and
catering facilities are available.
Visitors are welcome by
introduction or on application on
Monday and Friday.
Secretary: T McCracken — Tel:
03552 47728
Professional: J Taylor — Tel:
03552 22192

93 Edinburgh
Baberton Golf Club

Juniper Green, Edinburgh.
Tel: 031 453 4911.
18 holes, length of course 6140
yds.
SSS 69
Charges: £7 round, £10 daily.
For advance reservations Tel: 031
453 4911.
A practice area, caddy cars and
catering facilities are available.
Visitors are welcome weekdays by
arrangement.
Secretary: D M McBain — Tel:
031 453 4911
Professional: Mr K Kelly — Tel:
041 453 3555

★Braid Hills Golf Courses
Braid Hills Approach, Edinburgh
EH10.
18 x 2 holes, length of courses 5731
yds. and 4832 yds.
SSS 70 and 65
Visitors are welcome Monday to
Saturday.
(Further details on application)

The Bruntsfield Links Golfing Society

32 Barnton Mains, Edinburgh EH4.
Tel: 031 336 2006
18 holes, length of course 5824m/ 6707 yds.
SSS 70
Charges: On Application
For advance reservations Tel: 031 336 1479.
A practice area, caddy cars and catering facilities are available.
Secretary: M W Walton – Tel: 031 336 1479
Professional: Mr B McKenzie

★Carrick Knowe Golf Club

27 Glen Devon Park, Edinburgh.
Tel: 031 337 2217.
18 holes.
SSS 70
A practice area and catering facilities are available.
Visitors are welcome all week.
Secretary: Mr J B Wilkinson — Tel: 031 334 0932

★Craigentinny Golf Course

Craigentinny Avenue, Lochend, Edinburgh.
Tel: 031 554 7501
18 holes, length of course 5418 yds.
SSS (par 67)
Caddy cars available.
(Further details on application.)

Portobello Golf Club

Stanley Street, Edinburgh EH15.
Tel: 031 669 4361.
9 holes, length of course 2167m/ 2400 yds.
SSS 32
Charges: 95p round (9), £1.90 round (18).
For advance reservations Tel: 031 669 4361.
Visitors are welcome all week.
Secretary: Mr B Duffy — Tel: 031 669 2899

Duddingston Golf Club

Duddingston Road West, Edinburgh.
Tel: 031 661 7688
18 holes, length of course 6078m/ 6647 yds.
SSS 72
Charges: £6.90 round (Mon-Fri), £9.20 round (Sat/Sun), £8.05 daily.
(Charges subject to revision)
For advance reservations Tel: 031 661 7688.

A practice area, caddy cars and catering facilities are available.
Secretary: B P Underwood – Tel: 031 661 7688
Professional: Mr J Farmer

Kingsknowe Golf Club Ltd

326 Lanark Road, Edinburgh EH14 2JD.
Tel: 031 441 1145
18 holes, length of course 5469m/ 5979 yds.
SSS 69
Charges £4.50 round, £6.50 daily, £15 weekly.
For advance reservations Tel: 031 441 4030.
A practice area, caddy cars and catering facilities are available.
Visitors are welcome.
Secretary: H Hoddinott — Tel: 031 441 1145
Professional: W Bauld — Tel: 031 441 4030

Lothianburn Golf Club

106 Biggar Road
Edinburgh
Tel: 031 445 2206
SSS 69
Charges: £5 (weekday), £7 (weekend) round, £7 (weekday), £9.50 (weekend) daily.
For advance reservations Tel: 031 445 2288.
A practice area, caddy cars and catering facilities are available.
Visitors are welcome Monday to Friday.
Secretary: A R Roxton — Tel: 031 663 8354
Professional: B Mason — Tel: 031 445 2288

Merchants of Edinburgh Golf Club

10 Craighill Gardens, Edinburgh EH10 5PY.
Tel: 031 447 1219
18 holes, length of course 4889 yds.
SSS 65
Charges: £6 round, £8 daily, weekly terms on request.
For advance reservations Tel: 031 447 1219.
A practice area and catering facilities are available.
Visitors are welcome Monday to Friday.
Secretary: J B More — Tel: 031 443 1470
Professional: Mr G Jenkins — Tel: 031 447 8709

Mortonhall Golf Club

231 Braid Road, Edinburgh.
Tel: 031 447 2411
18 holes, length of course 5987m/ 6548 yds.
SSS 71
Charges on application.
Caddy cars and catering facilities are available.
Visitors are welcome by prior arrangement.

★Prestonfield Golf Club (Private)

6 Prestonfield Road North, Edinburgh.
Tel: 031 667 1273
18 holes, length of course 5685m/ 6216 yds.
SSS 70
Charges on application.
For advance reservations Tel: 031 667 8597.
A practice area, caddy cars and catering facilities are available.
Secretary: M D A G Dillon
Professional: Mr B Commins

★Silverknowes Golf Course

Silverknowes Parkway, Edinburgh EH4 5ET.
Tel: 031 336 3843
18 holes, length of course 6214 yds.
SSS 71
Visitors are welcome all week.

Ratho Park Golf Club

Ratho, Newbridge, Midlothian EH28 8NX.
Tel: 031 333 1252
18 holes, length of course 5514m/ 6028 yds.
SSS 69
Charges: £7 round, £9 daily, £12 weekend.
For advance reservations Tel: 031 333 1406.
A practice area, caddy cars and catering facilities are available.
Visitors are welcome Tuesday, Wednesday and Thursday.
Secretary: Mr A W McKinlay — Tel: 031 333 1752
Professional: Mr A Pate — Tel: 031 333 1406

Ravelston Golf Club

24 Ravelston Dykes Road, Edinburgh.
Tel: 031 332 3486
9 holes, length of course 4755m/ 5200 yds.
SSS Men 66, Ladies 69.
Catering facilities are available.

The Royal Burgess Golfing Society of Edinburgh
181 Whitehouse Road, Edinburgh EH4 6BY.
Tel: 031 339 3012
18 holes, length of course 6604 yds.
SSS 72
Charges: £16 round, £16 daily.
For advance reservations Tel: 031 339 6474.
A practice area, caddy cars and catering facilities are available. Visitors are welcome Monday to Friday.
Secretary: J Audis — Tel: 031 339 2075
Professional: G Yuille — Tel: 031 339 6474

Torphin Hill Golf Club
Torphin Road, Edinburgh EH13 0PG.
Tel: 031 441 1100
18 holes, length of course 5020 yds.
SSS 66
Charges: Daily - £4 weekdays, £7 weekends.
For advance reservations Tel: 031 441 1100.
A practice area and catering facilities are available.
Visitors are welcome all week (restrictions at weekends).
Secretary: D O Campbell — Tel: 031 441 1100

94 Edzell
By Brechin, Angus

The Edzell Golf Club
High Street, Edzell DD9 7TF.
Tel: 035 64 7283
18 holes, length of course 6299 yds.
SSS 70
Charges: Weekday £6 round, weekend £10 round, weekday £9 daily, weekend £10 daily, £30 weekly.
For advance reservations Tel: 035 64 7283.
A practice area, caddy cars and catering facilities are available (Caddies by arrangement).
Visitors are welcome all week.
Secretary: J M Hutchison — Tel: 035 64 7283
Professional: J B Webster — Tel: 035 64 462

95 Elderslie
Renfrewshire

Elderslie Golf Club
63 Main Road, Elderslie.
Tel: Johnstone 22835/23956
18 holes, length of course 5500m/6004 yds.
SSS 69
Charges: £6 round, £8 daily.
For advance reservations Tel: Johnstone 23956.
A practice area and catering facilities are available.
Secretary: W Muirhead – Tel: Johnstone 23956

96 Elgin
Morayshire

Elgin Golf Club
Hardhillock, Elgin IV30 3SX.
Tel: 0343 2338
18 holes, length of course 5853m/6401 yds.
SSS 71
Charges: £6 (weekday), £7 (weekend) round, £9 (weekday), £11 (weekend) daily.
For advance reservations Tel: 0343 2338/2884.
A practice area, caddy cars and catering facilities (except Tues) are available. (Caddies are available by arrangement with Professional).
Visitors are welcome all week.
Secretary: Mr Wm McKay — Tel: 0343 2338
Professional: Mr I Rodger — Tel: 0343 2884

97 Elie
Fife

Earlsferry Thistle Golf Club
Melon Park.
Tel: Anstruther 310053
(Further details on application)

'The Golf House Club'
Tel: Elie 330301/330327
18 holes, length of course 6253 yds.
SSS 70
Charges: £7 round (Mon-Fri), £8 (Sat/Sun), £10 daily (Mon-Fri), £12 (Sat/Sun).
Caddy cars and catering facilities are available.

98 Ellon
Aberdeenshire

McDonald Golf Club
Hospital Road, Ellon.
Tel: 0358 20576
18 holes, length of course 5473m/5986 yds.
SSS 69
Charges: £4.50 daily (Mon-Sat), £7 Sunday.
For advance reservations Tel: 0358 22891.
A practice area, caddy cars and catering facilities are available.
Visitors are welcome all week.
Secretary: Mr G Ironside — Tel: 0358 21961
Professional: Mr R Urquhart.

99 Eyemouth
Berwickshire

Eyemouth Golf Club
(Further details on application)

100 Falkirk
Stirlingshire

Falkirk Golf Club
Stirling Road, Camelon, Falkirk.
Tel: 0324 23457
18 holes, length of course 6090 yds.
SSS 69
Charges: £5 round, £7 daily.
Advance reservations by arrangement with secretary.
A practice area, caddy cars and catering facilities are available.
Visitors are welcome Monday to Friday up to 4.00p.m. (Parties — Mon/Tues/Thurs).
Secretary: A Bennie — Tel: 031 225 2092

★Grangemouth Golf Course
Polmont Hill, By Polmont.
Tel: Polmont 711500
18 holes, length of course 5796m/6339 yds.
SSS 71
Charges: £3 round (Mon-Fri), £4 (Sat/Sun), £5 daily.
For advance reservations Tel: Polmont 714355.
A practice area, caddy cars and catering facilities are available.
Secretary: Mr J Balfour
Professional: Mr J Black

101 Falkland
Fife

Falkland Golf Course
The Myre, Falkland.
Tel: Falkland 404
9 holes, length of course 2384m/
2608 yds.
SSS 66 (18)
Charges: £2.65 daily (Mon-Fri),
£4.20 (Sat/Sun).
Visitors are welcome by prior
arrangement.
Secretary: Mrs C R Forsythe –
Tel: Falkland 356

102 Fauldhouse
West Lothian

Greenburn Golf Club
Greenburn, Bridge Street,
Fauldhouse.
Tel: 0501 70292
18 holes, length of course 5676m/
6210 yds.
SSS 70
Charges: £4.00 round (Mon-Fri),
£6 (Sat/Sun), £6 daily (Mon-Fri),
£7.50 (Sat/Sun).
Advance reservations by
arrangement.
A practice area, caddy cars and
catering facilities are available.
Visitors are welcome all week.
Secretary: Mr A Morrison – Tel:
0501 70865
P.G.A. Professional: Mr D
Stevenson – Tel: 0501 71187

103 Fochabers
Morayshire

Garmouth & Kingston Golf Club
Garmouth, Fochabers.
Tel: 0343 87388
18 holes, length of course 5164m/
5649 yds.
SSS 67
Charges: £4 (weekdays) round, £5
(weekends) round, £4 (weekdays)
daily, £5 (weekends) daily.
For advance reservations Tel: 0343
87231.
Catering facilities are available.
Visitors are welcome all week.
Secretary: A Robertson — Tel:
0343 87231

104 Forfar
Angus

Forfar Golf Club
Cunninghill, Arbroath Road,
Forfar DD8 2RL.
Tel: 0307 62120

18 holes, length of course 5537
metres.
SSS 69
Charges: Daily — £8 (Mon - Fri),
£10.50 (Sat/Sun).
For advance reservations Tel: 0307
63773.
A practice area, caddy cars and
catering facilities are available.
Visitors are welcome all week.
Managing Secretary: A I C
Cameron — Tel: 0307 63773
Professional: Mr P McNiven —
Tel: 0307 65683

105 Forres
Morayshire

Forres Golf Club
Muiryshade, Forres.
Tel: 0309 72949
18 holes.
SSS 69
Charges: Summer £4, Winter £3
round, £6 daily, £16 weekly (5
days).
For advance reservations Tel: 0309
72949.
A practice area, caddy cars and
catering facilities are available.
Visitors are welcome all week.
Secretary: Mr G D Smith — Tel:
0309 72949
Professional: Mr J A Taylor —
Tel: 0309 72250

106 Fort Augustus
Inverness-shire

Fort Augustus Golf Club
Markethill, Fort Augustus.
Tel: Fort Augustus 6460
9 holes, length of course 5154
metres.
SSS 66
Charges: £3 round, £3 daily, £12
weekly (1986).
Caddy cars are available.
Visitors are welcome all week.
Secretary: I D Aitchison — Tel:
Fort Augustus 6460

107 Fortrose
Ross-shire

**Fortrose & Rosemarkie Golf
Club**
Ness Road East, Fortrose IV10
8SE.
Tel: Fortrose 20529
18 holes, length of course 5453m/
5973 yds.
SSS 69

Charges: £5.50 round, £5.50 (£7
Sat/Sun) daily, £22 weekly.
For advance reservations Tel:
Fortrose 20529 (parties only).
A practice area and caddies are
available.
Visitors are welcome all week.
Secretary: Margaret Collier — Tel:
Fortrose 20529
Professional G Hampton — Tel:
Fortrose 20733

108 Fort William
Inverness-shire

Fort William Golf Club
Torlundy, Fort William.
Tel: 0397 4464
18 holes, length of course 5160m/
5640 yds.
Charges: £4 round, £4 daily.
Snacks are available.
Visitors are welcome all week.
Secretary: Mr J Allan.

109 Fraserburgh
Aberdeenshire

Fraserburgh Golf Club
Philorth, Fraserburgh.
Tel: 0346 28287
18 holes, length of course 5688m/
6216 yds.
SSS 70
Charges: £4.30 daily (Mon-Fri),
£5.40 (Sat/Sun), £19.40 weekly.
A practice area and catering
facilities are available.
Secretary: Mr C A Chalmers –
Tel: 0346 28921

110 Gailes
By Irvine, Ayrshire

Glasgow Golf Club
Gailes, Irvine.
Tel: 0294 311347
18 holes, length of course 5896m/
6447 yds.
SSS 71
Charges: £15 round, £15 daily (To
be reviewed in December).
For advance reservations Tel: 041
942 2011.
A practice area, caddy cars and
catering facilities are available.
Caddies available by prior
arrangement.
Visitors are welcome Monday to
Friday (by prior arrangement).
Secretary: W D Robertson — Tel:
041 942 2011
Professional: Mr J Steven — Tel:
041 942 8507

111 Gairloch
Ross-shire

Gairloch Golf Club
Gairloch IV21 2BQ.
Tel: 0445 2407
9 holes, length of course (18 holes)
3540m/4186 yds.
SSS 63
Charges: £3 round, £5 daily, £15
weekly.
Caddy cars are available.
Visitors are welcome all week.
Secretary: W J Pinnell.

112 Galashiels
Selkirkshire

Torwoodlee Golf Course
Edinburgh Road.
Tel: Galashiels 2260
(Further details on application)

113 Galston
Ayrshire

Loudoun Golf Club
Galston.
Tel: 0563 820 551
18 holes, length of course 5323m/
5821 yds.
SSS 68
Charges: £8 daily.
For advance reservations Tel: 0563
821 993.
A practice area and catering
facilities are available.
Visitors are welcome Monday to
Friday.
Secretary: Mr C A Bruce, TD –
Tel: 0563 821 993

114 Gatehouse of Fleet
Kirkcudbrightshire

Gatehouse Golf Club
Gatehouse of Fleet.
Tel: Gatehouse 654
9 holes, length of course 2398 yds.
SSS 33
Charges: £4 round, £4 daily, £20
weekly.
For advance reservations Tel:
Gatehouse 654.
A practice area is available.
Visitors are welcome all week.
Secretary: E J Bryan — Tel:
Gatehouse 654.

115 Gifford
East Lothian

Gifford Golf Club
c/o Secretary, Cawdor Cottage,
Station Road, Gifford EH41 4QL.
Tel: Gifford 267
9 and 11 Tees, length of course
5613 metres.
SSS 69
Charges: £4 round (Sat/Sun), £4
daily (Mon - Fri).
For advance reservations Tel:
Gifford 267 (parties only).
A small practice area is available.
Visitors welcome except Tuesdays
and Wednesdays from 4.00p.m.
and Sundays from 12 noon.
Secretary: A C Harrison — Tel:
Gifford 267.

116 Girvan
Ayrshire

★Girvan Municipal Golf Course
Girvan.
Tel: Girvan 4272
(Further details on application)

117 Glasgow

★Alexandra Park Golf Course
Alexandra Park, Denniston,
Glasgow.
Tel: 041 556 3711.
9 holes, length of course 2870 yds.
Charges: 90p Adults, 45p Junior
round.
For advance reservations Tel: 041
556 3711.
A practice area and catering
facilities are available.
Visitors are welcome all week.

Bishopbriggs Golf Club
Brackenbrae Road, Glasgow.
Tel: 041 772 1810
18 holes, length of course 5524m/
6041 yds.
SSS 69
Charges on application.
A practice area and catering
facilities are available.
Secretary: R D Locke, CA – Tel:
041 772 7381

Cathcart Castle Golf Club
Mearns Road, Glasgow G76 7YL.
Tel: 041 638 9449
18 holes, length of course 5330m/
5832 yds.

Cawder Golf Club
Cadder Road, Bishopbriggs.
2 x 18 holes, length of course
Cawder 5711m/6244 yds., Kein
5373m/5885 yds.
SSS 71 & 68
Charges: £10 daily.
For advance reservations Tel: 041
772 5167.
A practice area, caddy cars and
catering facilities are available.
Visitors are welcome Monday to
Friday.
Secretary: G T Stoddart – Tel: 041
772 5167
Professional: K Stevely — Tel: 041
772 7102

Cowglen Golf Club
301 Barrhead Road, Glasgow G43.
Tel: 041 632 0556
18 holes, length of course 5465m/
5976 yds.
SSS 69
Charges: £7 (Introduction only)
round, £10 daily.
For advance reservations Tel: The
Secretary 0292 266600.
A practice area, caddies and
catering facilities are available.
Visitors are welcome Monday to
Friday.
Secretary: R J G Jamieson C.A.
— Tel: 0292 266600
Professional: J McTear — Tel: 041
649 9401

Crow Wood Golf Club
Garnkirk Estate, Muirhead,
Chryston G69 9JF.
Tel: 041 779 2011
(Further details on application)

★Deaconsbank Golf Course
Rouken Glen Park, Glasgow.
Tel: 041 638 7044
(Further details on application)

Haggs Castle Golf Course
70 Dumbreck Road, Glasgow.
Tel: 041 427 0480
(Further details on application)

Keir Golf Course
Cawder Golf Club
Tel: 041 772 7101
(Further details on application)

Glasgow Golf Club
Killermont, Bearsden, Glasgow.
Tel: 041 942 2011
18 holes, length of course 5456m/
5968 yds.
SSS 69

Charges: £15 round, £15 daily. (Charges to be reviewed in December 1986).
For advance reservations Tel: 041 942 2011.
A practice area and catering facilities are available.
Visitors are welcome by introduction on weekdays only.
Secretary: W D Robertson — Tel: 041 942 2011
Professional: Mr J Steven — Tel: 041 942 8507

Kings Park Golf Course
Crosspark Avenue, Glasgow.
Tel: 041 637 1066
(Further details on application)

★Knightswood Golf Course
Loanfoot Avenue, Knightswood.
Tel: 041 959 2131
(Further details on application)

★Lethamhill Golf Course
Hogganfield, Glasgow.
Tel: 041 770 8143
(Further details on application)

★Linn Golf Course
Simshill Road, Glasgow G44.
Tel: 041 637 5871
(Further details on application)

★Littlehill Golf Course
Auchinairn Road, Bishopbriggs.
Tel: 041 772 1916
(Further details on application)

Mount Ellen Golf Club
Johnstone House, Johnstone Road, Gartcosh.
Tel: Glenboig 872277
(Further details on application)

Pollok Golf Club
90 Barrhead Road, Glasgow.
Tel: 041 632 4351/1080
(Further details on application)

★Ruchill Golf Course
Brassey Street, Glasgow.
Tel: 041 946 9728
(Further details on application)

118 Glenluce
Wigtownshire

Wigtownshire County Golf Club
Mains of Park, Glenluce, Newton Stewart.
Tel: Glenluce 420

18 holes, length of course 5226m/ 5715 yds.
SSS 68
Charges: £4.50 daily (weekdays), £5 (Sat or Sun), £20 weekly.
For advance reservations Tel: 058 13 532.
Catering facilities are available.
Visitors are welcome all week except Wednesday after 6p.m.
Secretary: R McCubbin — Tel: 058 13 277

119 Glenrothes
Fife

Glenrothes Golf Club
Golf Course Road, Glenrothes.
Tel: 0592 758686
Length of course 5984m/6444 yds.
SSS 71
Charges: £2.40 round (weekday), £3.40 (weekend).
For advance reservations Tel: 0592 754561 (Evenings).
A practice area and catering facilities are available.
Visitors are welcome all week.
Secretary: L D Dalrymple — Tel: 0592 754561

120 Glenshee
by Blairgowrie, Perthshire

Dalmunzie Golf Course
Tel: 025-085 224
9 holes, length of course 2036 yards.
SSS 62
Charges: £3 daily, under 15 half price, under 10 free. Weekly family ticket £36.00.
Catering and accommodation available.

121 Golspie
Sutherland

Golspie Golf Club
Ferry Road, Golspie.
Tel: Golspie 3266
18 holes, length of course 5347m/ 5852 yds.
SSS 68
Charges: £5 daily, £25 weekly, £30 fortnightly.
A practice area, caddy cars and catering facilities are available.
Secretary: A Mackintosh

122 Gourock
Renfrewshire

Gourock Golf Club
Cowal View, Gourock.
Tel: Gourock 31001
18 holes, length of course 5936m/ 6492 yds.
SSS 71
Charges on application.
A practice area and catering facilities are available.
Visitors are welcome Monday to Friday.
Secretary: Mr J F MacLauchlan – Tel: Gourock 33696
Professional: Mr R Collinson

123 Grantown on Spey
Morayshire

Grantown on Spey Golf Club
Tel: Grantown 2079
18 holes, length of course 5224m/ 5713 yds.
SSS 67
Charge: £5.50 round, £25 weekly.
A practice area, caddy cars and catering facilities are available.
Secretary: Mr A L McKenzie – Tel: Grantown 2749

124 Greenock
Renfrewshire

Greenock Golf Club
Forsyth Street, Greenock PA16 8RE.
Tel: 0475 20793
27 holes, length of course 5888 yds.
SSS 68
Charges: £7 round, £7 daily, £18 weekly.
For advance reservations Tel: 0475 21435.
A practice area, caddy cars and catering facilities are available.
Visitors are welcome Tuesday, Thursday and Sunday.
Secretary: E J Black — Tel: 0475 20793
Professional: Mr K Murray — Tel: 0475 21435

125 Gullane
East Lothian

Gullane No 1 Golf Course
East Lothian EH31 2BB.
Tel: 0620 842255

18 holes, length of course 5935m/
6491 yds.
SSS 71
Charges: £13 round (Mon-Fri), £16
(Sat/Sun), £20 daily (Mon-Fri),
£24 (Sat/Sun), £75 weekly.
For advance reservations Tel: 0620
84 2255.
A practice area, caddy cars,
caddies and catering facilities are
available.
Visitors are welcome Monday to
Friday.
Secretary: J S Kinnear — Tel:
0620 842255
Professional: J Hume — Tel: 0620
843111

Gullane No 2 Golf Course
East Lothian EH31 2BB.
Tel: 0620 842255
18 holes, length of course 5603m/
6127 yds.
SSS 69
Charges: £6.50 round (Mon-Fri),
£7.50 (Sat/Sun), £9.50 daily (Mon-
Fri), £11.50 (Sat/Sun), £35 weekly.
For advance reservations Tel: 0620
842255.
A practice area, caddy cars,
caddies and catering facilities are
available.
Visitors are welcome all week.
Secretary: J S Kinnear — Tel:
0620 842255
Professional: J Hume — Tel: 0620
843111

Gullane No 3 Golf Course
East Lothian EH31 2BB.
Tel: 0620 842255
18 holes, length of course 4604m/
5035 yds.
SSS 64
Charges: £4.50 round (Mon-Fri),
£5.50 (Sat/Sun), £6.50 daily (Mon-
Fri), £7.50 (Sat/Sun), £25 weekly.
For advance reservations Tel: 0620
842255.
A practice area, caddy cars,
caddies and catering facilities are
available.
Visitors are welcome all week.
Secretary: J S Kinnear — Tel:
0620 842255
Professional: J Hume — Tel: 0620
843111

**The Honourable Company of
Edinburgh Golfers**
Muirfield, Gullane, East Lothian
EH31 2EG.
18 holes, length of course 6601
yds. (Medal Tees).
SSS 73

Charges: £22 round, £33 daily.
For advance reservations Tel: 0620
842123.
A practice area, caddy cars,
caddies and luncheon facilities are
available.
Visitors are welcome Tuesday and
Thursday (all day) and Friday
mornings.
Secretary: Major J G Vanreenen
— Tel: 0620 842123

126 Haddington
East Lothian

Haddington Golf Club
Amisfield Park, Haddington.
Tel: 062 082 3627/2727
18 holes, length of course 5764m/
6280 yds.
SSS 70
Charges: £4.50 round (Mon-Fri),
£5.75 (weekends), £6 daily (Mon-
Fri), £8.50 (weekends).
For advance reservations Tel: 062
082 3627.
A practice area, caddy cars and
catering facilities are available.
Visitors are welcome all week.
Secretary: J Shaw — Tel: 062 082
3627
Professional: G Muir — Tel: 062
082 2727

127 Hamilton
Lanarkshire

Hamilton Golf Club
(Further details on application)

128 Hawick
Roxburghshire

Minto Golf Club
Denholm, Hawick.
Tel: 0450 87220
18 holes, length of course 4992m/
5460 yds.
SSS 68
Charges: £5 round, £5 daily, £20
weekly.
For advance reservations Tel: 0450
72267/87220.
A practice area, caddy cars and
catering facilities are available.
Visitors are welcome all week.
Secretary: Mrs E Mitchell — Tel:
0450 72180
Professional: D Dunlop — Tel:
0835 62686

129 Helensburgh
Dunbartonshire

Helensburgh Golf Club
25 East Abercromby Street,
Helensburgh.
Tel: Helensburgh 4173
18 holes, length of course 5455m/
5966 yds.
SSS 69
Charges: £6 round, £8 daily.
A practice area, caddy cars and
catering facilities are available.
Secretary: R C McKechnie
Professional: Mr B Anderson

130 Helmsdale
Sutherland

Helmsdale Golf Club
Golf Road, Helmsdale KW8 6JA.
Tel: 043 12 240
9 holes, length of course 3650 yds
(2 x 9 holes).
SSS 62
Charges: £2 round, £2 daily, £7
weekly.
For advance reservations Tel: 043
12 240.
Visitors are welcome all week.
Secretary: Mr J Mackay — Tel:
043 12 240

131 Hopeman
Morayshire

Hopeman Golf Club
Hopeman, Moray.
Tel: Hopeman 830578
18 holes, length of course 4973m/
5439 yds.
SSS 66
Charges: £3.50 round (Mon-Fri),
£4.50 (Sat/Sun), £18 weekly.
For advance reservations Tel:
Hopeman 830578.
A practice area, and catering
facilities are available.
Visitors are welcome all week.
Secretary: Violet McPherson —
Tel: Hopeman 830444

132 Huntly
Aberdeenshire

Huntly Golf Club
Cooper Park, Huntly.
Tel: 0466 2643
18 holes, length of course 5399
yds.
SSS 66

Charges: £5 round (Mon-Fri), £6 (Weekends), £5 daily (Mon-Fri), £6 (weekends), £20 weekly.
For advance reservations Tel: 0466 3638.
Caddy cars and catering facilities are available.
Visitors are welcome all week.
Secretary: Mr G Angus — Tel: 0466 3638

133 Innellan
Argyllshire

Innellan Golf Club
Innellan.
Tel: Innellan 242
9 holes, length of course 18 holes 4246m/4642 yds.
Charges: £3 round, £3 daily, £12 weekly.
Catering facilities are available.
Visitors are welcome all week except Mon, Tues and Wed from 5.p.m.
Secretary: C Clark — Tel: Innellan 446

134 Innerleithen
Peeblesshire

Innerleithen Golf Course
Leithen Water.
9 holes, length of course 5318m/5820 yds.
SSS 68
Charges: £2.50 daily (Mon-Fri), £3.50 (Sat/Sun), £12 weekly.
Secretary: A F Watson – Tel: Innerleithen 830 774

135 Inverallochy
Aberdeenshire

Inverallochy Golf Course
24 Shore Street, Cairnbulg.
Tel: Inverallochy 2544
(Further details on application)

136 Invergordon
Ross-shire

Invergordon Golf Club
(Further details on application)

137 Inverness
Inverness-shire

Inverness Golf Club
Culcabock Road, Inverness IV2 3XQ.
Tel: 0463 239882

18 holes, length of course 5694m/6226 yds.
SSS 70
Charges: £8 (weekdays), £10 (Sundays and Public Holidays), £25 weekly (1986).
For advance reservations Tel: 0463 231989.
A practice area, caddy cars, caddies and catering facilities are available.
Visitors are welcome all week.
Secretary: Mr C D Thew — Tel: 0463 239882
Professional: A P Thomson — Tel: 0463 231989

138 Inverurie
Aberdeenshire

Inverurie Golf Club
Davah Wood, Blackhall Road, Inverurie.
Tel: Inverurie 20207/24080
18 holes, length of course 5182m/5667 yds.
SSS 68
Charges: £4 daily (Mon-Fri), £6 (Sat/Sun).
A practice area (for members only), caddy cars and catering facilities (except Mondays) are available.
Administrator: Mr J Skinner – Tel: Inverurie 24080

139 Irvine
Ayrshire

The Irvine Golf Club
Bogside, Irvine.
Tel: Bogside 75979
18 holes, length of course 5901m/6454 yds.
SSS 71
Charges: £7.50 round, £10 daily (under review).
For advance reservations Tel: Bogside 75979.
A practice area, caddy cars and catering facilities are available (Caddies by arrangement).
Visitors are welcome Monday to Thursday by arrangment.
Secretary: Mr Angus MacPherson — Tel: Bogside 75979
Professional: Mr Keith Erskine — Tel: Bogside 75626

★Ravenspark Golf Course
Kidsneuk.
Tel: Irvine 79550
18 holes.
SSS 71

Charges: 80p round, £1.10 daily, £6.50 weekly.
Caddy cars and catering facilities are available.
Visitors are welcome all week except Saturdays.
Secretary: W McMahon
Professional: Mr P Bond

140 Jedburgh
Roxburghshire

Jedburgh Golf Club
Dunion Road, Jedburgh.
9 holes, length of course 5492 yds.
SSS 67
Charges: £4 round/daily (Mon-Fri), £5 (Sat/Sun), weekly by arrangement with Secretary.
For advance reservations Tel: Jedburgh 63770.
Catering facilities are available (weekdays by prior arrangement only).
Visitors are welcome.
Secretary: N White — Tel: Jedburgh 63770

141 Johnstone
Renfrewshire

Cochrane Castle Golf Club
Craigston, Johnstone.
Tel: Johnstone 20146
18 holes, length of course 6226 yds.
SSS 70
Charges: £6 round, £9 daily.
For advance reservations Tel: Johnstone 20146.
A practice area, caddy cars and catering facilities are available.
Visitors are welcome Monday to Friday.
Secretary: J C Cowan — Tel: Johnstone 20146
Professional: T C Steele — Tel: Johnstone 28465

142 Keith
Banffshire

Keith Golf Course
Fife Park.
Tel: Keith 2469
18 holes, length of course 5253m/5745 yds.
SSS 68
Charges on application.

143 Kelso
Roxburghshire

Kelso Golf Club
Racecourse Road, Kelso.
Tel: 0573 23009
18 holes, length of course 5547m/
6066 yds.
SSS 69
Charges: On Application.
Catering facilities are available.
Visitors are welcome all week.
Secretary: Mr A Walker

144 Kemnay
Aberdeenshire

Kemnay Golf Club
Monymusk Road, Kemnay.
Tel: 0467 42225
9 holes.
SSS 60
Charges: £3 daily, £15 weekly.
For advance reservations Tel: 0467
42740.
Catering facilities are available.
Visitors are welcome Monday to
Saturday (Sundays with member).
Secretary: Mr P Hayward — Tel:
0467 42740

145 Kenmore
Perthshire

Taymouth Castle Golf Course
Kenmore.
Tel: 08873 228
18 holes, length of course 6066
yds.
SSS 69
Charges: £7 round (Mon-Fri), £9
(Sat/Sun), £10 daily (Mon-Fri),
£13 (Sat/Sun), £30 weekly (5
days).
For advance reservations Tel:
08873 228.
A practice area, caddy cars, petrol
buggy and catering facilities
available. (Caddies on prior
request).
Visitors welcome all week.
Golf Director/Professional A
Marshall — Tel: 08873 228

146 Kilbirnie
Ayrshire

Kilbirnie Place Golf Club
Largs Road, Kilbirnie.
Tel: Kilbirnie 683398
18 holes, length of course 5411
yds.
SSS 67

Charges: £4.50 round, £8 daily,
£20 weekly.
For advance reservations Tel:
Kilbirnie 683398.
A practice area and catering
facilities are available.
Visitors are welcome all week
except Saturday.
Secretary: J Thompson — Tel:
Kilbirnie 684317

147 Killin
Perthshire

Killin Golf Club
Killin Golf Course
Killin.
Tel: Killin 312
9 holes, length of course 2410 yds.
SSS 65
Charges: £2.50 round (after
6p.m.), £4 daily, £24 weekly.
(1986).
Caddy cars and catering facilities
are available.
Visitors are welcome all week.
Secretary: Mr J Blyth — Tel:
Killin 234

148 Kilmacolm
Renfrewshire

Kilmacolm Golf Club
Porterfield Road, Kilmacolm.
Tel: Kilmacolm 2139
18 holes, length of course 5964
yds.
SSS 68
Charges: £8 round, £12 daily.
For advance reservations Tel:
Kilmacolm 2139.
A practice area, caddy cars and
catering facilities are available.
Visitors are welcome Tues, Weds
and Thurs.
Secretary: R F McDonald — Tel:
Kilmacolm 2139
Professional: D Stewart — Tel:
Kilmacolm 2695

149 Kilmarnock
Ayrshire

★Caprington Golf Club
Ayr Road, Kilmarnock.
Tel: Kilmarnock 21915
(Further details on application)

150 Kilspindie
East Lothian

Kilspindie Golf Club
Tel: Aberlady 216
18 holes, length of course 4957m/
5176 yds.
SSS 66
Charges: £5.50 round (Mon-Fri),
£8 (Sat/Sun), £8 daily (Mon-Fri),
£12 (Sat/Sun).
Caddy cars and catering facilities
are available.
Visitors are welcome Monday to
Friday.
Secretary: J Thompson – Tel:
Aberlady 358 or 0620 2546

151 Kilsyth
Stirlingshire

Kilsyth Lennox Golf Club
(Further details on application)

152 Kincardine on Forth
Fife

Tulliallan Golf Club
Alloa Road, Kincardine-on-Forth.
Tel: Kincardine-on-Forth 30396.
(Further details on application)

153 Kingarth
Isle of Bute

Bute Golf Club
Kingarth.
9 holes, length of course 2284m/
2497 yds.
SSS 64
Charges: Adults £2 daily, £9
weekly, £18 fortnightly, Juniors
(under 17 yrs) 50p daily, £2 p.a.
Secretary: J Connell

154 Kinghorn
Fife

Kinghorn Municipal Golf Course
c/o Kirkcaldy District Council,
Dept. of Leisure and Recreation,
Kinghorn.
Tel: Kirkcaldy 61144
18 holes, length of course 4769m/
5216 yds.
SSS 67
Charges: £2.20 round (Mon-Fri),
£3.20 (Sat/Sun).
Catering facilites (except
Saturday) are available.
Secretary: D MacKenzie – Tel:
Kinghorn 890 345/890 157

155 Kingussie
Inverness-shire

Kingussie Golf Club
Gynack Road, Kingussie.
Tel: Clubhouse Kingussie 374/Sec.
Office Kingussie 600.
18 holes, length of course 5033m/
5504 yds.
SSS 67
Charges: £4 round, £5 daily, £22
weekly (1986).
For advance reservations Tel:
Kingussie 600/374.
Caddy cars and catering facilities
available.
Visitors are welcome all week.
Secretary: N D MacWilliam —
Tel: Kingussie 600

156 Kinnesswood
Kinross-shire

Bishopshire Golf Course
(Further details on application

157 Kinross
Kinross-shire

Green Hotel Golf Course
Green Hotel.
Tel: Kinross 63467
18 holes, length of course 6111m/
6655 yds.
SSS 70
Charges: £5 round (Mon-Fri), £8
(Sat/Sun), £8 daily (Mon-Fri), £12
(Sat/Sun).
For advance reservations Tel:
Green Hotel.
Caddy cars and catering facilities
are available.

158 Kintore
Aberdeenshire

Kintore Golf Club
(Further details on application)

159 Kirkcaldy
Fife

★Dunnikier Park Golf Course
Dunnikier Way, Kirkcaldy, Fife.
Tel: Kirkcaldy 261599
18 holes, length of course 5944m/
6501 yds.
SSS 72
Charges: £2.20 round (Mon-Fri),
£3.20 (Sat/Sun).

A practice area and caddy cars are
available.
Secretary: Mr D R Caird

Kirkcaldy Golf Club
Balwearie Road, Kirkcaldy, Fife.
Tel: Kirkcaldy 260370
18 holes, length of course 6004
yds.
SSS 70
Charges: £14 round (Weekdays),
£15 (weekends), £7 daily
(weekdays), £8.50 daily
(weekends).
For advance reservations Tel:
Kirkcaldy 266597/203258.
A practice area, caddy cars and
catering facilities are available.
Visitors are welcome all week
except Tuesdays and Saturdays.
Secretary: Mr Charles Taylor —
Tel: Kirkcaldy 266597
Professional: Mr Brian Lawson —
Tel: Kirkcaldy 203258

160 Kirkcudbright
Kirkcudbrightshire

Kirkcudbright Golf Club
Stirling Crescent, Kirkcudbright.
Tel: 0557 30314
18 holes, length of course 5121m/
5598 yds.
SSS 67
Charges: £5 round, £5 daily, £15
weekly.
For advance reservations Tel: 0557
30542.
Visitors are welcome all week.
Secretary: Mr A G Gordon — Tel:
0557 30542

161 Kirkintilloch
Dunbartonshire

Hayston Golf Club
Campsie Road, Kirkintilloch G66
1RN.
Tel: 041 776 1244
18 holes, length of course 5808m/
6042 yds.
SSS 69
Charges: £7 round, £12 daily.
For advance reservations Tel: 041
775 0882.
A practice area, caddy cars and
catering facilities are available.
Visitors are welcome on Tuesdays
and Thursdays.
Secretary: Mr J Weir — Tel: 041
339 7176
Professional: Mr R Graham —
Tel: 041 775 0882

Kirkintilloch Golf Club
Todhill, Campsie Road.
Tel: 041 776 1256
(Further details on application)

162 Kirkwall
Orkney

Orkney Golf Club
Grainbank.
Tel: Kirkwall 2457
(Further details on application)

163 Kirriemuir
Angus

Kirriemuir Golf Club
Northmuir, Kirriemuir.
Tel: 0575 72144
18 holes, length of course 5591
yds.
SSS 67
Charges: £7.50 daily, £20 weekly.
For advance reservations Tel: 0575
72729.
Caddy cars and catering facilities
are available.
Visitors are welcome weekdays.
Secretary: Fox & Irvine — Tel:
0575 72729
Professional: Mr A Caira — Tel:
0575 73317

164 Ladybank
Fife

Ladybank Golf Club
Annsmuir, Ladybank.
Tel: 0337 30814/30725
18 holes, length of course 6617
yds.
SSS 72
Charges: £8 round (weekdays),
£10 (weekends), £12 daily
(weekdays), £15 (weekends), £30
weekly.
For advance reservations Tel: 0337
30814.
A practice area, caddy cars and
catering facilities are available.
Visitors are welcome all week,
except Saturdays.
Secretary: D Downie — Tel: 0337
30814
Professional: Mr M Gray — Tel:
0337 30725

165 Lamlash
By Brodick, Isle of Arran

Lamlash Golf Club
Tel: Lamlash 296
18 holes, length of course 4280m/
4681 yds.
SSS 63
Charges: £3.50 daily, £17 weekly.
Secretary: E D R Pointer — Tel:
Lamlash 555

166 Lanark
Lanarkshire

Lanark Golf Club
The Moor, Whitelees Road,
Lanark.
Tel: Lanark 3219
18 hole and 9 hole, length of
course 6423 yds.
SSS 71 (18 hole)
Charges: £8 round, £12 daily (1986
inc. VAT).
For advance reservations Tel:
Lanark 2349.
A practice area, caddy cars and
catering facilities are available
(Caddies if requested).
Visitors are welcome Monday to
Friday.
Secretary: W W Law — Tel:
Lanark 3219
Professional: R Wallace — Tel:
Lanark 61456

167 Langbank
Renfrewshire

Gleddoch Golf & Country Club
Langbank PA14 6YE.
Tel: Langbank 304
18 holes, length of course Medal
Tees 6250, Forward Tees 5653.
SSS Medal Tees 71, Forward Tees
67.
Charges: £8 round (Mon-Fri),
£11.50 daily (Mon-Fri), £15
(weekend).
For advance reservations Tel:
Langbank 304.
A practice area, caddy cars and
catering facilities are available.
Visitors are welcome all week
except when club competitions are
on.
Secretary: G A Gordon — Tel:
Langbank 304
Professional: Mr K Campbell —
Tel: Langbank 704

168 Langholm
Dumfriesshire

Langholm Golf Course
Whitaside.
(Further details on application)

169 Larbert
Stirlingshire

Falkirk Tryst Golf Club
86 Burnhead Road,
Stenhousemuir, Larbert FK5 4QP.
Tel: 0324 562415
18 holes, length of course 5533
metres.
SSS 69
Charges: £5 round, £7 daily.
For advance reservations Tel: 0324
562050.
A practice area, caddy cars and
catering facilities are available.
Visitors are welcome Mon, Tues,
Thurs & Fri.
Secretary: Mr J J Weir — Tel:
0324 562050
Professional: Mr D Slicer — Tel:
0324 562091

Glenbervie Golf Club
Stirling Road, Larbert FK1 4SJ.
Tel: Larbert 562605
18 holes, length of course 6469
yds.
SSS 71
Charges: £9 per round (£14 for 2),
£14 daily.
For advanced reservations Tel:
Larbert 562605 (visiting parties).
A practice area, caddy cars and
catering facilities are available.
Visitors are welcome Monday to
Friday.
Secretary: Mrs M Purves — Tel:
Larbert 562605
Professional: Mr G McKay — Tel:
Larbert 562825

170 Largs
Ayrshire

Largs Golf Club
Irvine Road, Largs KA30 8EV.
Tel: 0475 673594
18 holes, length of course 6220
yds.
SSS 70
Charges: £7 round, £11 daily.
For advance reservations Tel: 0475
686192.
A practice area, caddy cars and
catering facilities are available.

Visitors are welcome all week.
Secretary: F Gilmour — Tel: 0475
672497
Professional: R Stewart — Tel:
0475 686192

171 Larkhall
Lanarkshire

★Larkhall Golf Course
(Further details on application)

172 Lauder
Berwickshire

★Lauder Golf Course
Tel: Lauder 409
(Further details on application)

173 Lennoxtown
Stirlingshire

Campsie Golf Course
Crow Road.
Tel: Lennoxtown 310244
(Further details on application)

174 Lenzie
Lanarkshire

Lenzie Golf Club
19 Crosshill Road.
Tel: 041 776 1535
18 holes, length of course 5465m/
5977 yds.
SSS 69
Charges: £5 round, £7.50 daily.
For advance reservations Tel: 041
776 1535.
A practice area, caddy cars and
catering facilities are available.
Secretary: A W Jones — Tel: 041
776 1535
Professional: K McKechnie

175 Lerwick
Shetland

The Shetland Golf Club
Dale Golf Course
P O Box 18.
Tel: Gott 369
18 holes, length of course 5460m/
5971 yds.
SSS 71
Charges: £3 daily (Mon-Fri), £4
(Sat/Sun).
Caddy cars are available.
Visitors are welcome.
Secretary: Mr A P Gordon

176 Leslie
Fife

Leslie Golf Club
(Further details on application)

177 Lesmahagow
Lanarkshire

★Hollandbush Golf Club
Acretophead, Lesmahagow.
Tel: Lesmahagow 893484
18 holes, length of course 6110 yds.
SSS 70
Charges: £4 daily (weekdays), £6 (weekend)
For advance reservations Tel: Lesmahagow 893646.
A practice area, caddy cars and catering facilities are available.
Visitors are welcome all week.
Secretary: Mr J Hamilton — Tel: Coalburn 222
Professional: Mr I Rae — Tel: Lesmahagow 893646

178 Leuchars
Fife

St. Michael's Golf Club
Tel: Leuchars 365
SSS 67 (par 70).
(Further details on application)

179 Leven
Fife

Leven Links Golf Course
Leven Links
Tel: Leven 23509
18 holes, length of course 5800m/ 6400 yds.
SSS 71
Charges: £6 round (weekdays), £7 (weekends), £9.50 daily (weekdays), £10.50 (weekends), £22 (weekly).
For advance reservations Tel: Leven 23509.
Caddy cars and catering facilities are available.
Visitors are welcome Sunday to Friday.
Secretary: Mr M Innes — Tel: Leven 23509

Leven Thistle Golf Club
Balfour Street, Leven.
Tel: Leven 23798

18 holes, length of course 5800m/ 6434 yds.
SSS 71
Charges: £7 round, £9.50 daily.
For advance reservations Tel: Mr M Innes Leven 23509.
A practice area, caddy cars and catering facilities are available.
Visitors are welcome Monday to Friday (Small Parties — weekend).
Secretary: J Scott — Tel: Leven 23798

★Scoonie Golf Course
North Links.
(Further details on application)

180 Linlithgow
West Lothian

Linlithgow Golf Club
Braehead, Linlithgow.
Tel: Linlithgow 842585
18 holes, length of course 5359m/ 5858 yds.
SSS 68
Charges: £5 round (Mon-Fri), £7 round (Sat/Sun), £7 daily (Mon-Fri), £9 daily (Sat/Sun).
For advance reservations Tel: Linlithgow 844356.
A practice area, caddy cars and catering facilities are available.
Visitors are welcome all week except Wednesdays and Saturdays.
Secretary: J T Menzies TD — Tel: Linlithgow 842585
Professional: Mr D Smith — Tel: Linlithgow 844356

181 Lochcarron
By Strathcarron, Ross-shire

Lochcarron Golf Club
Lochcarron.
Tel: 05202 291
9 holes, length of course 3466 yards (18).
Charges: £1 round, £1 daily, £5 weekly.
For advance reservations Tel: 05202 291
A practice area is available.
Visitors are welcome all week.
Secretary: Mr J Borland — Tel: 05202 291

182 Lochgelly
Fife

Lochgelly Golf Course
Lochgelly Golf Club
Cartmore Road.
Tel: Lochgelly 780174
18 holes, length of course 5022m/ 5492 yds.
SSS 66
Charges: £3 round (Mon-Fri), £4.25 (Sat/Sun), £5 daily (Mon-Fri), £7.25 (Sat/Sun).
Catering facilities are available on Sundays.
Secretary: R F Stuart — Tel: Cowdenbeath 512238

183 Lochgilphead
Argyllshire

Lochgilphead
Blarbuie Road, Lochgilphead.
Tel: 0546 2340
9 holes, length of course 4484 yds.
SSS 63
Charges: £3 daily (weekdays), £5 (weekends).
For advance reservations Tel: 0546 2149.
Visitors are welcome all week.
Secretary: P W Tait — Tel: 0546 2149

184 Lochmaben
By Lockerbie, Dumfriesshire

Lochmaben Golf Club
Back Road, Lochmaben.
Tel: Lochmaben 552
(Further details on application)

185 Lochranza
Isle of Arran

Lochranza Golf Course
(Further details on application)

186 Lockerbie
Dumfriesshire

Lockerbie Golf Club
Corrie Road, Lockerbie.
Tel: Lockerbie 3363
18 holes, length of course 5418 yds.
SSS 66
Charges: £5 daily, £20 weekly.
For advance reservations Tel: Lochmaben 274.

A practice area, and catering facilities by arrangement are available.
Visitors are welcome all week.
Secretary: R Barclay — Tel: 038 781 274

187 Lochwinnoch
Renfrewshire

Lochwinnoch Golf Club
Burnfoot Road, Lochwinnoch.
Tel: Lochwinnoch 842153
(Further details on application)

188 Longniddry
East Lothian

Longniddry Golf Club
Tel: Longniddry 52141
(Further details on application)

189 Lossiemouth
Morayshire

Moray (Old) Moray (New) Golf Club
Stotfield, Lossiemouth.
Tel: Lossiemouth 2018
Two courses 18 holes, length of courses (Old) 6075m/6643 yds, (New) 5526m/6044 yds.
SSS (Old) 72, (New) 69.
Charges: (Old) £7 daily (weekdays), £10 (weekends), £30 weekly, (New) £5 daily (weekdays), £6 (weekends), £20 weekly.
For advance reservations Tel: Lossiemouth 2018.
Caddy cars and catering facilities are available.
Visitors are welcome to (New) all week, (Old) Monday to Friday.
Secretary: Mr J Hamilton — Tel: Lossiemouth 2018
Professional: Mr A Thomson — Tel: Lossiemouth 3330

190 Lundin Links
Fife

Lundin Golf Club
Golf Road, Lundin Links, Leven.
Tel: Lundin Links 320202
18 holes, length of course 6377 yds.
SSS 71
Charges: £8 round (Mon-Fri), £12 daily (Mon-Fri), £35 weekly, £10 round Saturday only.

For advance reservations Tel: Lundin Links 320202.
A practice area, caddy cars (wide wheels only) and catering facilities except Mondays are available.
Visitors are welcome Monday to Saturday.
Secretary: A C McBride — Tel: Lundin Links 320202
Professional: D K Webster — Tel: Lundin Links 320051

Lundin Ladies Golf Club
Woodlielea Road, Lindin Links,
(Further details on application)

191 Lybster
Caithness

Lybster Golf Course
(Further details on application)

192 Macduff
Banffshire

Royal Tarlair Golf Club
Buchan Street, Macduff.
Tel: 0261 32897
18 holes, length of course 2719m/2968 yds.
SSS 68
Charges: £4 round, £6 daily (weekdays), £7 (weekends), £30 weekly.
For advance reservations Tel: 0261 32897.
Caddy cars and catering facilities are available.
Visitors are welcome all week.
Secretary: Mrs L Edwards — Tel: 0261 32897

193 Machrie
Port Ellen, Isle of Islay

The Machrie Golf Club
The Machrie Hotel & Golf Club, Port Ellen, Islay PA42 7AN.
Tel: 0496 2310
18 holes, length of course 5692m/6226 yds.
SSS 70
Charges: £7.50 round, £12 daily, £72 weekly.
For advance reservations Tel: 0496 2310.
A practice area, caddies, caddy cars and catering facilities are available.
Visitors are welcome all week.
Hotel & Golf Course Proprietor:
Mr M MacPherson.

194 Maddiston
By Falkirk, Stirlingshire

Polmont Golf Club Ltd
Manuelrigg, Maddiston.
Tel: Polmont 711277
9 holes, length of course 5567m/6088 yds.
SSS 69
Charges: £2 daily, £2.50 round (Sat), £3 round (Sun).
Catering facilities available on booking.
Secretary: Mr P Lees — Tel: Polmont 713811

195 Mallaig
Inverness-shire

Traigh Golf Club
(Further details on application)

196 Mauchline
Ayrshire

Ballochmyle Golf Course
Tel: 0290 50469
18 holes, length of course 5442m/5952 yds.
SSS 69
Charges: On Application.
Caddy cars and catering facilities are available.

197 Maybole
Ayrshire

★Maybole Golf Course
(Further details on application)

198 Melrose
Roxburghshire

Melrose Golf Club
The Clubhouse, Dingleton Road, Melrose.
Tel: Melrose 2855
9 holes, length of course 4996m/5464 yds.
SSS 68
Charges: £4 daily (weekdays), £5 daily (weekends).
Visitors are welcome all week.
Secretary: L M Wallace — Tel: Earlston 617

199 Millport
Isle of Cumbrae

Millport Golf Course
(Further details on application)

---

200 Milnathort
Kinross-shire

Milnathort Golf Club Ltd
South Street, Milnathort.
Tel: 0577 64069
9 holes, length of course 2959 yds.
SSS 68
Charges: £4 daily (weekdays), £5 daily (weekends).
For advance reservations Tel: 0577 64069.
A practice area and catering facilities are available.
Visitors are welcome all week.
Captain: W A S M Smith — Tel: 0577 62536

201 Milngavie
Dunbartonshire

Hilton Park Golf Club
Tel: 041 956 4657
18 x 2 holes.
Catering facilities available.
(Further details on application)

Dougalston Golf Club
Strathblane Road, Milngavie, Glasgow.
Tel: 041 956 5750
18 holes, length of course 6300m/6683 yds.
Charges: £4 round, £6 daily.
For advance reservations Tel: 041 956 5750.
A practice area, caddy cars and catering facilities are available.
Visitors are welcome all week.
Secretary: W McInnes — Tel: 041 956 5750
Professional: W Murray — Tel: 041 956 5750

Milngavie Golf Club
Laigh Park, Milngavie, Glasgow G62.
Tel: 041 956 1619
18 holes, length of course 5818 yds.
SSS 68
A practice area and catering facilities are available.
Visitors are welcome if introduced by a member.
Secretary: G Law — Tel: Duntocher 76286

202 Moffat
Dumfriesshire

The Moffat Golf Club
Coatshill Golf Course Road, Moffat DG10 9SB.
Tel: 0683 20020
18 holes, length of course 5218 yds.
SSS 66
Charges: £5 round (Mon-Fri), £7 daily (Mon-Fri), £9 (Sat/Sun), £28 weekly.
For advance reservations Tel: 0683 20020.
A practice area, caddy cars and catering facilities are available.
Visitors are welcome all week except Wednesdays.
Secretary: T A Rankin — Tel: 0683 20020

203 Monifieth
Angus

Broughty Golf Club
Princes Street, Monifieth.
Tel: Monifieth 532147
(Further details on application)

Medal Golf Course
The Links, Monifieth.
Tel: Monifieth 532767
(Further details on application)

Ashludie Golf Course
The Links, Monifieth.
Tel: Monifieth 2767
(Further details on application)

204 Montrose
Angus

Mercantile Golf Club
East Links, Montrose.
Tel: Montrose 72408
(Further details on application)

205 Motherwell
Lanarkshire

Colville Park Golf Club
Jerviston Estate, Merry Street, Motherwell.
Tel: Motherwell 63017
18 holes, length of course 5681m/6213 yds.
SSS 70 (par 71)
Charges: £7 daily.
For advance reservations Tel: Motherwell 63017/66045 (after 5p.m.).
A practice area and catering facilities are available.
Visitors are welcome by prior arrangement Monday to Friday.
Secretary: Mr E Wood — Tel: Motherwell 66045 (after 5p.m.)

206 Muckhart
By Dollar, Clackmannanshire

Muckhart Golf Club
Tel: Muckhart 423
18 holes, length of course 5589m/6112 yds.
SSS 70
Charges: £4 round (Mon-Fri), £6 (Sat), £6 daily (Mon-Fri), £8 (Sat/Sun).
Caddy cars and catering facilities are available.
Secretary: R T Glaister
Professional: Mr K Salmoni

207 Muir of Ord
Ross-shire

Muir of Ord Golf Club
Great North Road, Muir of Ord IV6 7SX.
Tel: 0463 870842
18 holes, length of course 5129 yds.
SSS 65
Charges: April/Sept £4 daily (weekdays), £5 (Sat/Sun), Oct/March £3 daily (weekdays), £4 (Sat/Sun), Summer £20 weekly.
For advance reservations Tel: 0463 870842.
A practice area and catering facilities are available.
Visitors are welcome all week.
Secretary: Mrs C Moir — Tel: 0463 870842
Professional: Mr J T Hamilton — Tel: 0463 870601

208 Musselburgh
East Lothian

The Musselburgh Golf Club
Monktonhall, Musselburgh.
Tel: 031 665 2005
18 holes, length of course 6630 metres.
SSS 72
Charges on request.
A practice area, caddy cars and catering facilities are available.
Visitors are welcome by arrangement.
Secretary: J R Brown — Tel: 031 553 1701
Professional: Mr T Stangoe — Tel: 031 665 7055

209 Muthill
Perthshire

Muthill Golf Club
Peat Road, Muthill,
Crieff PH5 2AD.
9 holes, length of course 2167m/
2371 yds.
SSS 63 (18 holes)
Charges: £3 daily (Mon-Fri), £3.50
(Sat/Sun).
Visitors are welcome (evenings
may be restricted for club
matches).
Secretary: W H Gordon — Tel:
0764 3319

210 Nairn
Nairn Golf Club

Seabank Road, Nairn.
Tel: 0667 53208
18 holes, length of course 6540
yds.
SSS 71
Charges: £9 round (Mon-Fri), £10
(Sat/Sun), £11 daily (Mon-Fri),
£12 (Sat/Sun), £40 weekly.
For advance reservations Tel: 0667
53208.
A practice area, caddies, caddy
cars and catering facilities are
available.
Visitors are welcome all week.
Secretary: Mr D Patrick — Tel:
0667 53208
Professional: Mr R Fyfe — Tel:
0667 52787

Nairn Dunbar Golf Club
Tel: Nairn 52741
18 holes, length of course 6431
yards.
SSS 71
Charges: £5 daily (Mon-Fri), £6
(Sat/Sun).
A practice area and caddy cars are
available.
Secretary: Mrs S J MacLennan
Professional: R Phimister

211 Nethybridge
Inverness-shire

Abernethy Golf Club
Tel: Nethybridge 204
9 holes, length of course 2271m/
2484 yds.
SSS 33
Charges: On Application.
A practice area and caddy cars are
available.

212 Newburgh-on-Ythan
Aberdeenshire

**Newburgh-on-Ythan Golf
Course**
(Further details on application)

213 New Cumnock
Ayrshire

New Cumnock Golf Club
(Further details on application)

214 New Galloway
Kirkcudbrightshire

New Galloway Golf Course
c/o Secretary.
Tel: New Galloway 239
9 holes, length of course 2294m/
2508 yds.
Charges on application.
Visitors are welcome (Booking in
advance).
Secretary: Mr D M Browning

215 Newton Mearns
Renfrewshire

**The East Renfrewshire Golf
Club**
Pilmuir.
Tel: Langswell 256
(Further details on application)

Eastwood Golf Club
Muirshield, Loganswell, Newton
Mearns, Glasgow G77 6RX.
Tel: Loganswell 261
18 holes, length of course 5886
yds.
SSS 68
Charges: £6.50 round, £10 daily.
(Subject to prior application and
approval).
For advance reservations Tel:
Loganswell 280.
Caddy cars and catering facilities
are available.
Visitors are welcome all week.
Secretary: C B Scouler — Tel:
Loganswell 280
Professional: K McWade — Tel:
Loganswell 285.

216 Newton Stewart
Wigtownshire

Newton Stewart Golf Club
Kirroughtree Avenue, Minnigaff,
Newton Stewart.
Tel: 0671 2172

9 holes.
For advance reservations Tel: 0671
2292.
Catering facilities are available.
Secretary: D F Buchanan — Tel:
0671 2292

217 Newtonmore
Inverness-shire

Newtonmore Golf Club
Tel: Newtonmore 328
18 holes, length of course 5890
yds.
SSS 68
Charges: £5 daily, £20 weekly.
Caddy cars and catering facilities
are available.

218 North Berwick
East Lothian

★East Links Golf Course
Tel: North Berwick 2726
(Further details on application)

★Glen Golf Club
East Links, Tantallon Terrace,
North Berwick.
Tel: 0620 2221
18 holes, length of course 5565m/
6086 yds.
SSS 69
Charges: £4.50 round, £6.50 daily.
For advance reservations Tel: 0620
2221.
A practice area, caddies, caddy
cars and catering facilities are
available.
Visitors are welcome all week.
Secretary: D R Montgomery —
Tel: 0620 2340
Professional: Mr D Huish

219 Oban
Argyllshire

Glencruitten Golf Course
Glencruitten Road, Oban.
Tel: Oban 62868
(Further details on application)

220 Old Meldrum
Aberdeenshire

Old Meldrum Golf Club
(Further details on application)

221 Paisley
Renfrewshire

★Barshaw Golf Club
Barshaw Park, Paisley.
Tel: 041 889 2708
(Further details on application)

The Paisley Golf Course
Tel: 041-884 2292
18 holes, length of course 5857m/
6424 yds.
SSS 71
Charges: £6 round, £8 daily.
A practice area and catering
facilities are available.
Secretary: W J Cunningham —
Tel: 041-884 3903

222 Peebles
Peebleshire

★Peebles Municipal Golf Course
Kirkland Street, Peebles.
Tel: Peebles 20153 (Ext. 220).
18 holes, length of course 5612m/
6137 yds.
SSS 69
Charges on application.
A practice area, caddy cars and
catering facilities are available.
Secretary: G Garvie

223 Penicuik
Midlothian

Glencorse Golf Club
Milton Bridge, Penicuik EH26
0RD.
Tel: Penicuik 76939
18 holes, length of course 5205
yds.
SSS 66
Charges: £5 round, £7 daily
(Subject to review).
For advance reservations Tel:
Penicuik 77189 (Clubs/Societies
only).
Caddy cars and catering facilities
are available.
Visitors are welcome on Mon,
Tues, Wed and Thursdays.
Secretary: D A McNiven — Tel:
Penicuik 77189
Professional: Mr C Jones — Tel:
Penicuik 76481

224 Perth
Perthshire

**The Craigie Hill Golf Club (1982)
Ltd**
Cherrybank, Perth.
Tel: 0738 24377/22644

18 holes, length of course 5379
yds.
SSS 66
Charges: £4 round (Mon-Fri), £6
daily (Mon-Fri), £8 (Sat/Sun).
For advance reservations Tel: 0738
22644.
A practice area, caddy cars and
catering facilities are available.
Visitors are welcome all week
except Saturdays.
Secretary: Mr W A Miller — Tel:
0738 22644
Professional: Mr F Smith — Tel:
0738 22644

King James VI Golf Club
Moncreiffe Island, Perth.
Tel: Perth 25170/32460
18 holes, length of course 5521m/
6037 yds.
SSS 69
Charges: £4.75 round, £7 daily
(Mon-Sat), £9.50 (Sun).
For advance reservations Tel:
Perth 32460.
A practice area, caddy cars and
catering facilities are available.

225 Peterhead
Aberdeenshire

**Craigewan Golf Course
Peterhead Golf Club**
Craigewan Links, Peterhead.
Tel: Peterhead 72149
18 holes, length of course 5550m/
6070 yds.
SSS 69
Charges: £4 daily (Mon-Fri), £7.50
(Sat/Sun).
A practice area and catering
facilities are available.
Secretary: Mr Wm G Noble

226 Pitlochry
Perthshire

Pitlochry Golf Course Ltd
Pitlochry Estates Office.
Tel: Pitlochry 2114
(Further details on application)

227 Port Glasgow
Renfrewshire

Port Glasgow Golf Club
Devol Road, Port Glasgow.
Tel: 0475 704181
18 holes, length of course 5592m/
5712 yds.
SSS 68

Charges: £5 round, £8 daily,
weekly by arrangement.
For advance reservations Tel: 0475
704181.
A practice area and catering
facilities are available.
Visitors are welcome uninvited
before 3.55p.m., not on Saturdays
and invited only Sundays.
Secretary: N L Mitchell — Tel:
0475 706273

228 Portmahomack
Ross-shire

Tarbat Golf Club
Portmahomack.
Tel: 0862 87 519
9 holes, length of course 4658 yds.
SSS 63
Charges: £2 daily, £8 weekly.
For advance reservations Tel:
Portmahomack 519.
A practice area, caddies and caddy
cars are available. Catering
facilities available at local hotels.
Visitors are welcome all week
except Sundays.
Secretary: Mr J R Long — Tel:
Portmahomack 519

229 Portpatrick
By Stranraer, Wigtownshire

Portpatrick (Dunskey) Golf Club
Tel: 0776 81 273
18 holes, (9 hole, par 3).
Charges: £6 daily (Mon-Fri), £7
(Sat/Sun), £20 weekly, £30
fortnightly.

230 Port William
Wigtownshire

St Medan Golf Club
Port William.
Tel: Port William 358
9 holes, length of course 2277 yds.
SSS 62
Charges: £4 round, £5 daily, £20
weekly.
Catering facilities are available.
Visitors are welcome all week.
Secretary: D O'Neill — Tel:
Whithorn 555

231 Prestonpans
East Lothian

Royal Musselburgh Golf Club
Preston Grange House,
Prestonpans.
Tel: Prestonpans 810 276

18 holes, length of course 5676 metres.
SSS 70
Charges: £6.50 round (Mon-Fri), £7.50 (Sat/Sun), £11 daily.
For advance reservations Tel: Prestonpans 810 139.
Caddy cars and catering facilities are available.
Visitors are welcome Monday to Friday (no visiting parties at weekends).
Secretary: Mr T H Hardie — Tel: Prestonpans 810 276
Professional: Mr A Minto — Tel: Prestonpans 810 139

232 Prestwick
Ayrshire

Old Prestwick Golf Course
Prestwick Golf Club
2 Links Road, Prestwick.
Tel: Prestwick 77404
18 holes, length of course 5983m/ 6544 yds.
SSS 72
Charges on application.
A practice area, caddies and caddy cars are available.
Visitors are welcome all week (except Saturdays and Public Holidays).
Secretary: J A Reid, CA
Professional: F C Rennie

Prestwick St Cuthbert Golf Club
East Road, Prestwick KA9 2SX.
Tel: 0292 77101
18 holes, length of course 6470 yds.
SSS 71
Charges: £7 round, £10 daily, £30 weekly.
For advance reservations Tel: 0292 77101.
A practice area and catering facilities (except Thursdays) are available.
Visitors are welcome Monday to Friday (not on weekends or public holidays).
Secretary: R M Tonner — Tel: 0292.77101

Prestwick St Nicholas Golf Club
Grangemuir Road, Prestwick KA9 15N.
Tel: 0292 77608
18 holes, length of course 5361m/ 5864 yds.
SSS 68

Charges: £9 round (after 2p.m.), £14 daily.
For advance reservations Tel: 0292 77608.
Caddy cars and catering facilities are available.
Visitors are welcome Monday to Friday only.
Secretary: J C Wallace — Tel: 0292 77608
Professional: I Parker — Tel: 0292 79755

233 Pumpherston
West Lothian

Pumpherston Golf Club
Drumshoreland Road, Pumpherston.
Tel: Livingston 32869
(Further details on application)

234 Reay
By Thurso, Caithness

Reay Golf Club
Tel: Reay 288
18 holes, length of course 5372m/ 5876 yds.
SSS 68
Charges: £4 round, £4 daily, £15 weekly.
A practice area is available.
Secretary: J A Marsh — Tel: Thurso 63035

235 Renfrew
Renfrewshire

Renfrew Golf Club
Blythswood Estate, Inchinnan Road, Renfrew.
Tel: 041 886 6692
18 holes, length of course 6227m/ 6812 yds.
SSS 73
Charges: £5.50 round, £9 daily.
Catering services are available.
Secretary: I Park

236 Rigside
Lanarkshire

Douglas Water Golf Club
(Further details on application)

237 Rothesay
Isle of Bute

★Port Bannatyne Golf Club
Bannatyne Mains Road, Port Bannatyne.
Tel: 0700 2009

13 holes, length of course 4256m/ 4654 yds.
SSS 63
Charges: £2 daily, £3 (weekends), £10 weekly.
For advance reservations Tel: 0700 2009.
Visitors are welcome all week.
Secretary: Mr I L MacLeod — Tel: 0700 2009

Rothesay Golf Course
Miwisters Brae, Rothesay.
Tel: 0700 2244
18 holes, length of course 5370 yds.
SSS 67
Charges: £4 daily (Mon-Fri), £5.50 (Sat/Sun), £16 weekly.
For advance reservations Tel: 0700 3554.
A practice area, caddy cars and catering facilities are available.
Visitors are welcome all week.
Secretary: Mr D Shaw — Tel: 0700 2244
Professional: Mr G McKinlay — Tel: 0700 3554

238 Rutherglen
Lanarkshire

Blairbeth Golf Club
Fernhill, Rutherglen.
Tel: 041 634 3355
18 holes, length of course 4982m/ 5448 yds.
SSS 67
Charges: £5 daily.
For advance reservations Tel: 041 632 0604.
A practice area and catering facilities are available.
Secretary: F T Henderson – Tel: 041 632 0604

239 St Andrews
Fife

Royal & Ancient Golf Club
Tel: St. Andrews 72112/3
(Further details on application)

St Andrews Old Course
18 holes, length of course 6566 yds.
SSS 72
Charges: £16.50 round all week (closed Sunday).
For advance reservations Tel: St. Andrews 75757.

Caddies and caddy cars are available.
Executive Secretary: A Beveridge — Tel: St. Andrews 75757

St Andrews New Course
18 holes, length of course 6039m/6604 yds.
SSS 72
Charges: £7 round, all week; £35 7 day ticket (unlimited play).
For advance reservations Tel: St. Andrews 75757.
Caddies and caddy cars are available.
Executive Secretary: A Beveridge — Tel: St. Andrews 75757

St Andrews Eden Course
18 holes, length of course 5460m/5971 yds.
SSS 69
Charges: £6 round, all week; £35 7 day ticket (unlimited play).
For advance reservations Tel: St. Andrews 75757.
Caddies and caddy cars are available.
Executive Secretary: A Beveridge — Tel: St. Andrews 75757

St Andrews Jubilee Course
18 holes, length of course 6284 yds.
SSS 70
Charges: £4 round, all week: £35 7 day ticket (unlimited play).
Caddies and caddy cars available.
Executive Secretary: A Beveridge — Tel: St. Andrews 75757

St Andrews Balgove Course
9 holes.
Charges: £1.50 per round (18 holes).
Children's & beginner's course.
Executive Secretary: A Beveridge – Tel: St. Andrews 75757
(Further details on application)

240 St Boswells
Roxburghshire

St Boswells Golf Club
St. Boswells, Roxburghshire.
Tel: 0835 22359
9 holes, length of course 5054 yds.
SSS 65
Charges: £3 round, £3 daily, £12 (5 days), £15 (7 days).

For advance reservations Tel: 0835 22359.
Visitors are welcome all week.
Secretary: G B Ovens — Tel: 0835 22359

241 St Fillans
Perthshire

St Fillans Golf Club
South Lochearn Road, St Fillans.
Tel: St Fillans 312
9 holes, length of course 4812m/5268 yds.
SSS 66
Charges: £3 daily (Mon-Fri), £4 (Sat/Sun), £15 weekly.
Caddy cars and limited catering facilities are available.
Visitors are welcome all week.
Secretary: Mr R A Brown — Tel: St Fillans 302

242 Saline
Fife

Saline Golf Club
Kinneddar Hill, Saline.
Tel: 0383 852 591
9 holes, length of course 5308 yds.
SSS 66
Charges: £3 daily (Mon-Fri), £4 (Sat/Sun).
A practice area and catering facilities are available.
Visitors are welcome all week except Saturdays.
Secretary: R Hutchison — Tel: 0383 852 344

243 Sanquhar
Dumfriesshire

Euchan Golf Course
Sanquhar.
Tel: 06592 577
9 holes, length of course 5144 metres.
SSS 68
Charges: £5 round (Mon-Fri), £8 (Sat/Sun), £5 daily.
For advance reservations Tel: 06592 324.
A practice area and catering facilities (advance notice by parties) are available.
Visitors are welcome all week.
Secretary: D A Hamilton — Tel: 06592 206

244 Scarinish
Isle of Tiree

Vaul Golf Club
(Further details on application)

245 Sconser
Isle of Skye

Sconser Golf Club
(Further details on application)

246 Selkirk
Selkirkshire

Selkirk Golf Club
Selkirk Hills, Selkirk.
Tel: Selkirk 20621
(Further details on application)

247 Shotts
Lanarkshire

Blairhead Golf Course
Shotts Golf Club
Blairhead, Shotts.
Tel: Shotts 20431
(Further details on application)

248 Skelmorlie
Ayrshire

Skelmorlie Golf Course
Tel: Wemyss Bay 520152
(Further details on application)

249 Southend
By Campbeltown, Argyllshire

Dunaverty Golf Club
(Further details on application)

250 Southerness
Kirkcudbrightshire

Southerness Golf Club
Southerness, Dumfries DG2 8AZ.
Tel: 0387 88 677
18 holes, length of course 6551 yds.
SSS 72
Charges: £8 daily (Mon-Fri), £10 (Sat/Sun), £30 weekly.
For advance reservations Tel: 0387 53588.
A practice area, caddy cars and catering facilities are available.
Visitors are welcome all week.
Secretary: W T Train — Tel: 0387 53588

251 South Uist
Western Isles

Links-Land Golf Course
Askernish Golf Club
Askernish.
Tel: Lochboisdale 258
9 holes (18 tees), length of course
5312 yds.
SSS 67
Charges: £2 daily, £10 weekly.

252 Spey Bay
Morayshire

Spey Bay Golf Club
Tel: Fochabers 820424
(Further details on application)

253 Stevenston
Ayrshire

Ardeer Golf Club
Greenhead, Stevenston.
Tel: 0294 64542
18 holes, length of course 6630
yds.
SSS 72
Charges: £8 daily (weekdays), £11
Sundays, £35 weekly.
For advance reservations Tel: 0294
64035.
A practice area, caddy cars and
catering facilities are available.
Visitors are welcome all week
except Saturdays.
Secretary: Mr Wm T Burnett —
Tel: 0294 64035

254 Stirling
Stirlingshire

Stirling Golf Club
Queen's Road, Stirling FK8 2QY.
Tel: Stirling 73801
18 holes, length of course 6409
yds.
SSS Medal 71, Front Tee 69.
Charges: £6.50 round, £10 daily.
A practice area, caddy cars and
catering facilities are available.
Visitors are welcome all week.
Asst. Secretary: Mrs L C Sayer —
Tel: Stirling 64098
Professional: Mr J Chillas — Tel:
Stirling 71490

255 Stonehaven
Kincardineshire

Stonehaven Golf Club
Cowie, Stonehaven AB3 2RH.
Tel: Stonehaven 62124
18 holes, length of course 4669m/
5103 yds.
SSS 65
Charges: £6 daily (Mon-Fri), £7.50
(Sat/Sun), £24 weekly.
For advance reservations Tel:
Stonehaven 62124.
A practice area and catering
facilities are available.
Visitors are welcome Monday to
Friday, Late afternoon and
evening on Saturday and Sunday.
Secretary: Mr R M Murdoch —
Tel: Stonehaven 62124

256 Stornoway
Isle of Lewis

Stornoway Golf Course
Tel: Stornoway 2240
18 holes, length of course 4681m/
5119 yds.
SSS 66
Charges: £4 round, £6 daily, £20
weekly.
No Sunday golf.
For advance reservations Tel:
Stornoway 2570.
Caddy cars and catering facilities
are available.
Secretary: Mr D W M Duggie —
Tel: Stornoway 2570

257 Stranraer
Wigtownshire

★Stranraer Golf Club
Creachmore, By Stranraer.
Tel: Leswalt 245
18 holes, length of course 5760m/
6300 yds.
SSS 71
Charges: £4.75 round (Mon-Fri),
£6.30 (Sat/Sun), £6.30 daily (Mon-
Fri), £9.50 (Sun), £25.25 weekly.
A practice area, caddy cars and
catering facilities are available.
Secretary: Mr W I Wilson — Tel:
Stranraer 3539

258 Strathaven
Lanarkshire

Strathaven Golf Club
Overton Avenue, Glasgow Road,
Strathaven.
Tel: Strathaven 20422
18 holes, length of course 5696m/
6226 yds.
SSS 70
Charges: £6.50 round, £10 daily.
For advance reservations Tel:
Strathaven 20421.
A practice area, caddy cars and
catering facilities are available.
Secretary: Mr G Fleming — Tel:
Strathaven 20421
Professional: Mr M McCrorie

259 Strathpeffer
Ross-shire

Strathpeffer Spa Golf Club
Strathpeffer IV15 9AS.
Tel: 0997 21219
18 holes, length of course 4000m/
4813 yds.
SSS 65
Charges: £4.50 daily, £18 weekly.
For advance reservations Tel: 0997
21219.
A practice area, caddy cars and
catering facilities are available.
Visitors are welcome all week.
Secretary: Mr N Roxburgh — Tel:
0997 21396

260 Strathtay
By Pitlochry, Perthshire

Strathtay Golf Course
9 holes, length of course 1774m/
1940 yds.
SSS 63
(Further details on application)

261 Stromness
Orkney

Stromness Golf Club
Ness, Stromness.
Tel: Stromness 850593
18 holes, length of course 4762
yds.
SSS 64
Charges: £4 round, £4 daily.
Bar facilities are available.
Visitors are welcome all week.
Secretary: F J Groundwater —
Tel: 0856 850622

262 Tain
Ross-shire

Tain Golf Club
Tel: Tain 2314
(Further details on application)

263 Tarbert
Argyllshire

Tarbert Golf Course
Kilberry Road, Tarbert.
Tel: 08802 565
9 holes, length of course 4460 yards.
SSS 64
Charges: £3 round, £5 daily, £20 weekly.
For advance reservations Tel: 08802 565/676.
Visitors are welcome all week.
Secretary: Mr J B Sinclair — Tel: 08802 676

264 Tarland
Aberdeenshire

Tarland Golf Club
Tel: Tarland 413
(Further details on application)

265 Tayport
Fife

Scotscraig Golf Club
Golf Road, Tayport DD6 9DZ.
Tel: 0382 552515
18 holes, length of course 6486 yds.
SSS 71
Charges: £7 round (Mon-Fri), £8.50 (Sat/Sun), £11.50 daily (Mon-Fri), £13 (Sat/Sun), £25 weekly (5 days).
For advance reservations Tel: 0382 552515.
A practice area, caddy cars and catering facilities (not full catering on Tuesdays) are available.
Visitors are welcome all week.
Secretary: 0382 552515

266 Thornhill
Dumfriesshire

Thornhill Golf Course
(Further details on application)

267 Thornton
Fife

Thornton Golf Club
Tel: Glenrothes 771111
18 holes, length of course 5648m/6177 yds.
SSS 69
Charges: £4 round (Mon-Fri), £6 (Sat/Sun), £6 daily (Mon-Fri), £9 (Sat/Sun).
Catering facilities are available.
Secretary: M Moss — Glenrothes 754240

268 Thurso
Caithness

Thurso Golf Club
Newlands of Geise, Thurso.
Tel: Thurso 63807
18 holes, length of course 5319m/5818 yds.
SSS 69
Charges: £4 daily (Mon-Fri), £5 (Sat/Sun), £20 weekly.
Catering facilities are available.
Secretary: G Bailey

269 Tighnabruaich
Argyllshire

Kyles of Bute Golf Club
Tel: 0700 811 355
9 holes, length of course 2379 yds.
SSS 66
Charges: £2.50 daily.
Secretary: D W Gieve

270 Tillicoultry
Clackmannanshire

Tillicoultry Golf Course
Alva Road, Tillicoultry.
9 holes, length of course 4518m/5266 yds.
SSS 66
Charges: £2.50 daily (Mon-Fri), £5 (Sat/Sun).
For advance reservations Tel: Tillicoultry 51337.
A practice area and catering facilities are available.
Visitors are welcome all week (except competition days).
Secretary: Mr R Whitehead — Tel: 0259 51337

271 Tobermory
Isle of Mull

Western Isles Golf Course
9 holes, length of course 4922 yds.
Charges: £3 daily, £12 weekly.
(Further details on application)

272 Torphins
Aberdeenshire

Torphins Golf Club
(Further details on application)

273 Troon
Ayrshire

Royal Troon Golf Club
Old Course, Craigend Road, Troon KA10 6EP.
Tel: Troon 311555
18 holes, length of course 6641 yds.
SSS 73
Charges: £18 daily.
Caddies, Caddy cars and catering facilities are available.
Visitors are welcome Monday to Friday.
Secretary: J A Sword

Royal Troon Golf Club
Portland Course, Craigend Road, Troon KA10 6EP.
Tel: Troon 311555
18 holes, length of course 6274 yds.
SSS 71
Secretary: J A Sword

★Lochgreen Golf Course
Tel: Troon 312464
18 holes, length of course 6188m/6765 yds.
SSS 72
(Further details on application)

★Darley Golf Course
Tel: Troon 312464
18 holes, length of course 5817m/6327 yds.
SSS 70
(Further details on application)

★Fullarton Golf Course
St Meddans Golf Club
Harling Drive, c/o Director, Parks and Recreation Dept., Kyle and Carrick District Council, 30 Miller Road, Ayr.
Tel: Ayr 81511 (Ext. 249).
18 holes, length of course 4632m/5064 yds.
(Further details on application)

274 Turnberry
Ayrshire

Arran & Ailsa
Turnberry Hotel & Golf Courses
Tel: Turnberry 202
18 x 2 holes, length of course
Arran 5738m/6276 yds., Ailsa
5841m/6388 yds.
SSS Arran 70, Ailsa 71.
A practice area, a driving range,
caddies, caddy cars and catering
facilities are available.
Professional: Mr B Jamieson

275 Turriff
Aberdeenshire

Turriff Golf Club
Rosehall, Turriff.
Tel: 0888 62745
18 holes, length of course 5581m/
6105 yds.
SSS 69
Charges: £4.50 round (Mon-Fri),
£5.50 (Sat/Sun), £6 daily (Mon-
Fri), £7 (Sat/Sun).
For advance reservations Tel: 0888
68789/63025.
A practice area, caddy cars and
catering facilities are available.
Visitors are welcome all week.
Secretary: Mrs M MacRae — Tel:
0888 68789
Professional: Mr A Hemsley —
Tel: 0888 63025

276 Uddingston
Lanarkshire

Calderbraes Golf Club
57 Roundknowe Road,
Uddingston.
Tel: Uddingston 813425
(Further details on application)

277 Uphall
West Lothian

Uphall Golf Club
Tel: 0506 856404
(Further details on application)

278 West Calder
West Lothian

Harburn Golf Club
West Calder EH55 8RS.
Tel: West Calder 871256/871131
18 holes, length of course 5340m/
5843 yds.
SSS 68

Charges: £6 round (Mon-Fri),
£7.50 (Sat/Sun), £8.50 daily (Mon-
Fri), £10 (Sat/Sun).
For advance reservations Tel:
West Calder 871582.
A practice area, caddy cars and
catering facilities are available.
Visitors are welcome all week.
Secretary: G R Clark — Tel: West
Calder 871131
Professional: R Redpath — Tel:
West Calder 871582

279 West Kilbride
Ayrshire

West Kilbride Golf Club
Fullerton Drive, West Kilbride
KA23 9HT.
Tel: 0294 823042
18 holes, length of course 6247
metres.
SSS 70
Charges: £12 round, £12 daily, £40
weekly.
For advance reservations Tel: 0294
823042.
A practice area, caddy cars and
catering facilities are available.
Visitors are welcome Monday to
Friday.
Secretary: J Mitchell — Tel: 0294
823911
Professional: G Howie — Tel:
0294 823042

280 West Linton
Peebleshire

West Linton Golf Club
West Linton.
Tel: 0968 60463
18 holes, length of course 5336m/
5835 yds.
SSS 68
Charges: £5.50 round (Mon-Fri),
£6.50 (Sat/Sun), £7.50 daily (Mon-
Fri), £9 (Sat/Sun).
For advance reservations Tel: 0968
60256
A practice area and catering
facilities are available.
Visitors are welcome all week
except Sundays.
Secretary: S Hunter OBE — Tel:
0968 60373
Professional: Mr D Stewart — Tel:
0968 60256

281 Westray
Orkney

Westray Golf Club
(Further details on application)

282 Whiting Bay
Isle of Arran

Whiting Bay Golf Club
Tel: 07707 487
18 holes, length of course 4405
yds.
SSS 63
Charges: £4 daily, £17 weekly.
Catering facilities are available.
Secretary — Tel: 07707 305

283 Wick
Caithness

Wick Golf Club
Reiss By Wick.
Tel: (0995) 2726
18 holes, length of course 5976
yds.
SSS 69
Charges: £4 round, £4 daily, £15
weekly, £24 monthly.
For advance reservations Tel:
(0995) 2726
A practice area is available.
Visitors are welcome all week.
Acting Secretary: A R Barker —
Tel: (0995) 2726

284 Wigtown
Wigtownshire

Wigtown & Bladnoch Golf Club
(Further details on appliction)

285 Wishaw
Lanarkshire

Wishaw Golf Club
55 Cleland Road, Wishaw.
Tel: Wishaw 372869
18 holes, length of course 5609m/
6134 yds.
SSS 69
Charges: £7 daily (Mon-Sat), £10
(Sun).
A practice area, caddy cars and
catering facilities are available.
Secretary: I Scott
Professional: J Campbell

Mileage Chart

The distances between towns on the mileage chart are given to the nearest mile, and are measured along the normal AA recommended routes. It should be noted that AA recommended routes do not necessarily follow the shortest distances between places but are based on the quickest travelling time, making maximum use of motorways or dual-carriageway roads.

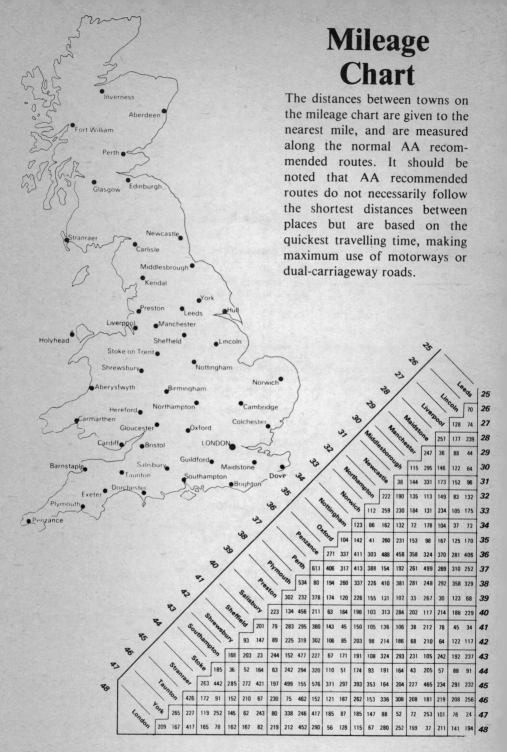

Mileage chart (distances read to each destination listed across the diagonal: Leeds, Lincoln, Liverpool, Maidstone, Manchester, Middlesborough, Newcastle, Northampton, Norwich, Nottingham, Oxford, Penzance, Perth, Plymouth, Preston, Salisbury, Sheffield, Shrewsbury, Southampton, Stoke, Stranraer, Taunton, York, London):

From \ To	Leeds	Lincoln	Liverpool	Maidstone	Manchester	Middlesborough	Newcastle	Northampton	Norwich	Nottingham	Oxford	Penzance	Perth	Plymouth	Preston	Salisbury	Sheffield	Shrewsbury	Southampton	Stoke	Stranraer	Taunton	York
Lincoln	70																						
Liverpool	128	74																					
Maidstone	257	177	239																				
Manchester	247	36	88	44																			
Middlesborough	115	295	146	122	64																		
Newcastle	38	144	331	173	152	96																	
Northampton	222	190	135	113	149	83	132																
Norwich	112	259	230	184	131	234	105	175															
Nottingham	123	66	162	132	72	178	104	37	72														
Oxford	104	142	41	260	231	153	98	167	125	170													
Penzance	271	337	411	303	488	458	358	324	370	281	406												
Perth	611	406	317	413	388	154	192	261	499	269	310	252											
Plymouth	534	80	194	260	337	226	410	381	281	248	292	358	329										
Preston	302	232	378	174	120	226	155	131	102	33	267	30	123	68									
Salisbury	223	134	456	211	63	164	196	103	313	284	202	117	214	188	229								
Sheffield	201	79	283	295	360	143	45	150	105	136	106	38	212	78	45	34							
Shrewsbury	93	147	89	225	319	302	106	85	203	98	214	186	68	210	64	122	117						
Southampton	168	203	23	244	152	477	227	67	191	108	324	293	231	105	242	192	237						
Stoke	185	36	52	164	63	242	294	320	110	51	174	93	191	164	43	205	57	88	91				
Stranraer	263	442	285	272	421	197	499	155	576	371	297	393	353	164	204	227	465	234	291	232			
Taunton	426	172	91	152	210	67	230	75	462	152	121	187	262	153	336	308	208	181	219	208	256		
York	265	227	119	252	145	62	243	80	338	246	417	185	87	185	147	88	52	72	253	101	76	24	
London	209	167	417	165	78	162	167	82	219	212	452	290	56	128	115	67	280	252	199	37	211	141	194

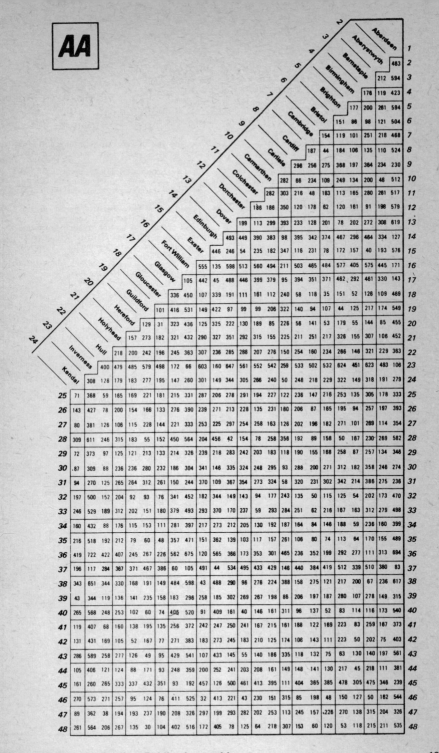

Enjoy Scotland for Golf

C. MILLER

Scotland is a land full of golf courses — nearly five hundred for a country with a population of only 4 million. They are also unique in that, with few exceptions, all welcome visiting golfers.

Now 28 privately owned independent hotels in Scotland who banded together several years ago as Inter Hotel Scotland have pooled their experience to offer Stay and Enjoy Scotland golfing holidays designed to give quality accommodation at good value for money prices and at the same time, make booking easy. All that is required is one call on a 24 hour service, a letter or telex and a staff of experienced advisors are there to help you at no extra cost. Scotland, wherever you go, takes time to discover and to avoid the stress of living out of a suitcase Stay and Enjoy Scotland holidays are primarily designed on a 3-5-7 night no rush basis with free advice and ideas on wherever you wish to go and want to do.

Whichever part of Scotland you visit you will find an Enjoy Scotland Holiday Hotel and nearby will be a golf course or more likely a selection of golf courses. Put your clubs in the back of your car and just drive, from Auchan Castle near Moffat, Tweed Valley close to Peebles or Corsemalzie House in Wigtownshire — all in the south — to Dornoch in the far north, or St Andrews on the east coast.

However, for the "afficionado" there are the special areas and special courses for which more time is needed even a week or two weeks, and Inter Hotel Scotland has a special list of these.

You can choose one or two centres for short breaks or as many as you wish for longer golfing holidays, touring out each day to discover the area. Each hotel as well as offering welcome and hospitality will give you advice on places of interest, scenic routes, castles, gardens, shopping, crafts and activities including fishing, riding, walking, birdwatching arts and many more as well as golf.

Pre-booking arrangements are to be advised in Scotland even for increasingly popular off-season breaks. Stay and Enjoy Scotland holidays are all booked ensuring rooms with bath or shower and toilet en suite and most provide extras including tea and coffee tray, colour television, radio, telephone and hairdryers.

Enjoy Scotland

A lot of care has gone into planning these no-rush holidays which offer more than touring, sightseeing and activities.

For the family there are special concession prices and children sharing with two adults have free accommodation.

Special occasions have been thought of and on arrival or for an anniversary during your holiday, a surprise welcome including champagne and flowers can be arranged at any of the hotels — ideal for honeymoons or birthdays.

Taste of Scotland Holidays are part of the scheme for those who enjoy good food and wish to savour a selection of local and traditional Scottish dishes.

Special terms have been arranged in the scheme for car-hire if required, together with air and rail travel link-up information for both home and overseas visitors. Insurance arrangements are also on hand at concession rates for UK residents.

These location holidays which begin with a minimum of three nights at any one centre can be extended as long as is wished. For instance you can make up a seven day holiday with three nights in one area and four in another, or stay at one hotel. The longer you stay at one hotel, the cheaper the rate becomes and the rates are adjusted for good value in both low and high season. High season dates are 14th May to 30th September.

The 1987 rates per person, per night sharing a twin or double room with bath include VAT. No service charge is made for any of these holidays and gratuities are purely at guests discretion.

	HIGH SEASON	LOW SEASON
3 Nights:	£32.75	£28.50
5 Nights:	£31.25	£27.75
7 Nights:	£29.75	£26.00

Even stop-over nights en route are offered at bed and breakfast rates for one or two nights.

Enjoy Scotland

All the hotels are privately owned and most of them are run by the owners themselves and their families. Although they have grouped together they do not belong to one large company controlled and supervised by a head office.

Inter Hotels in Scotland are individual, none of them are alike and this is one of their attractions.

When you stay in an Inter Hotel, whether by the sea or lochside, in the country or in the town, you will receive the welcome and hospitality for which Scotland is famous.

For further information and booking ring, write or telex and say you have read Scotland Home of Golf.

Stay and Enjoy Scotland
Booking and Advise Service
Room
2d Churchill Way
Bishopbriggs,
Glasgow G64 2RH
Phone: 041-762 0838
Telex 777205 INSCOT G